AHA!

AHA!

a puzzle approach to creative thinking

Morgan Worthy

Nelson Hall Chicago

Library of Congress Cataloging in Publication Data

Worthy, Morgan.
    Aha! : A puzzle approach to creative thinking.

    1. Creative thinking.   2. Puzzles. I. Title.
BF408.W67   153.3'5   75-23143
ISBN 0-88229-271-4   9-14-76

Manufactured in the United States of America

Dedication

For my wife, Polly Hammond Worthy, and our children, Bonnie and Steve.

Contents

Acknowledgments

My wife, Polly Hammond Worthy, has been a valued coworker in each step of the original development of training materials and in the preparation of the manuscript. I am also indebted to my colleagues James Dabbs, Sandra Gibson, and Shelia Kessler for reading the manuscript and making many helpful suggestions. Susan Katz, Diane Kistner, and Gail Mitchell gave valuable assistance in the preparation of the manuscript. Most of all, I am indebted to the students, friends, and workshop participants who have tried this approach, given me feedback on their experiences, and, in many individual cases, encouraged me to make the materials available in published form.

Introduction

We are all gods. We each create from time to time. You, no doubt, have had the experience of suddenly seeing a better way of doing something that you had done many times before. Your new and better way, perhaps important only to you, was no less an act of creation than the sudden insights of artists, writers, inventors, scientists, or others who are engaged in "creative" endeavors. You and I clearly profit from our ability to do creative thinking, and each of us can improve that ability by understanding the creative process and nurturing that process in our own thinking.

This introduction will not be a full discussion of the creative process. For those who wish to read such an account, I recommend Arthur Koestler's excellent book, *The Act of Creation: A Study of the Conscious and*

Unconscious in Science and Art. My purpose here is merely to introduce a point of view about what are central elements in creative thinking and to provide a rationale for the use of aha! puzzles as a way to illustrate, stimulate, and cultivate that manner of thinking. Lest that prospect sound too forbidding, and seem to involve a lot of work, let me say from the outset that creative people think of their work as play, and, anyway, puzzles are meant to be fun. They are not to be worked; they are to be played.

What Is Creative Thinking?

Many people confuse original thinking with creative thinking. Original thinking involves ideas or responses that are uncommon. Creative thinking also requires that one's ideas or responses be uncommon or atypical but, in addition, they must be recognized as somehow better than the old, accustomed, typical response. Providing a new answer to an old question is not a sign of creative thinking unless the new answer can be seen as somehow better than the old. Creative bursts of scientific breakthroughs are always characterized by a new theoretical answer to an old question that makes more sense of the known facts than did the old answer. A creative invention involves a better tool, a better machine, a better design, a better process, a better something.

If asked, "What is 2 + 2?" I might answer 17. My answer would be highly original, but it would not be at all creative. It is a different answer, but it is not a better answer. I fear that this point is often missed by people who pride themselves on being different because they feel that this is the sure mark of a creative mind. In an analogous manner, change—whether political or personal—may be incorrectly perceived as "progress" when it is merely change—which can just as easily signal regression as progression. Difference, change, uncommonness, originality are not enough. A creative idea must work, fit, match, above all, solve the problem.

Unfortunately, schools spend little time trying to teach creative thinking. Even when the attempt is made, the emphasis is on originality rather than creativity. Learning to be original, or to let one's originality find expression, is important and worthwhile, but it is only the first step to becoming a creative thinker. If one is to be creative, he or she must learn to guide original thinking toward solutions, toward better fits, toward answers that are, in a real and verifiable sense, correct. The puzzles in this volume have "correct" answers which the person either discovers or fails to discover. Flexible, original, divergent thinking is required, but it is not treated as an end in itself; it is the means to the creative or correct solution.

Two Key Elements in Creativity

Many efforts have been made to discover how creative people differ from noncreative people. Numerous findings have been published. Clearly, intelligence is not the answer. A certain minimal level of intelligence is required for creative thinking, but beyond that point, I.Q. is a poor predictor of creative output. Many personality traits have been identified as being more common in creative people than in noncreative people of equal intelligence and education. Some of the traits that are often mentioned are independence, introversion, playfulness, and a sense of humor.

Other researchers have concentrated on the

creative process itself in an effort to see what it is that creative people do in their work that leads to creative output. Numerous observations have been made and various theories advanced. These can be reduced, I believe, to two key elements. I call these two key elements "fruitful obsession" and "aha! thinking." These characteristics are learned and can, I believe, be stimulated and developed through practice. Each of these elements will be considered briefly.

Fruitful Obsession

Whenever we study the lives of great thinkers, scientists, inventors, or others famous for their creative output, we find that these people allowed themselves to become completely caught up in their own area of creative endeavor. This might have involved a particular question or problem on which that person thought, worked, pondered—perhaps for years. To those who observed this behavior, the individual might have seemed a bit strange or egocentric in the total preoccupation with his or her own particular interest, whatever it was. This is obsession—the preoccupation with a particular idea or sphere of interest. Some forms of obsession are pathological. The paranoid is obsessed with suspicions that people are plotting against him. The depressed person is obsessed with morbid thoughts such as death. Such obsessions are not usually fruitful or creative.

Fruitful obsession can be as intense, as all-consuming, as the pathological variety, but we make a mistake if we think of obsessions as unusual, and foreign to our own experience. Each of us has or has had obsessions of one kind or another. For one it is stamp-collecting, for another, baseball, detective stories, or flying saucers, and for yet another, it is how to make a buck, find a mate, or build a better mousetrap. In each case, there is an intense interest which focuses our perception, increases our store of particular knowledge, and prepares us for *possible* creative insights that would never occur with a less focused or prepared mind. Obsession does not necessarily, or even usually, lead to creative insights of great value, but obsession does make them possible.

Studying the lives of creative people reveals over and over again the importance and power of healthy obsession. The person first becomes absorbed in some question, some goal, some preoccupation, some challenge, and from that, in time, flow the creative insights, the leap to new knowledge, the scientific breakthrough, the revolutionary invention, the better answer to an old question. Reading the lives of men such as Freud, Darwin, or Edison makes us aware of the tremendous power of an active, directed, goal-oriented obsession. Our obsessions may well be less intense and the creative fruits of our obsessions less important to the world, but whatever our creative potential, we will realize it, in part, to the degree that we find our own "magnificent obsession."

I am convinced of the power of obsession because of what I have read about others, but I am more convinced by what I know to be true in my own life. I am a research psychologist and, as such, being productive and, hopefully, creative, is very important to me. During the last few years, I have become obsessed with a particular research question, and that obsession has led to scientific results exceeding anything I had accomplished before. The question, to me an exciting one, is what relationship eye color has to behavior. Behavioral scientists had more or less ignored eye color as a predictor of behavior and assumed that the color of a person's eyes could be of interest to a songwriter, perhaps, but not to a scientist. That view, which I shared, was suddenly changed for me one day when I happened to notice (aha!) that, among professional football players, there was a relationship between eye color of the player and the position played—the darker-eyed players being in those positions that require the most speed. The implications of this discovery and the challenge of finding other relationships between eye color and behavior so intrigued me, so challenged me, that I dropped everything else I was doing and gave my new obsession full rein. I lived, ate, and gave up sleep for my eye-color obsession, not because I had to, but because I wanted to.

The obsession paid off in more findings. By looking at other sports, I noted a tendency for light-eyed players to be most successful on tasks that do not require speed, but do require delayed or unhurried responses. For example, in professional baseball, light-eyed players, as a group, do better as pitchers than as hitters; dark-eyed players, as a group, do better as hitters. By looking at the hunting tactics of birds of prey and other animal predators I noted similar differences. Dark-eyed species tend to use tactics that require speed and quick reactions; light-eyed species more often use tactics such as stalking or ambush that require hesitation or delay of response.

Much more research will have to be done before the various connections between eye color and behavior are completely verified and fully understood. My point here is only to illustrate how a good obsession can be fruitful. I published a book on my findings, and now other behavioral scientists are becoming more interested in this area of research. I have had the pleasure of discussing my eye-color work on national radio and television programs, and it has received wide coverage in newspapers and magazines.[1] The degree that my efforts to be a creative researcher have been successful, I attribute, in part, to a willingness to drop everything and become fully obsessed with a question that had, to use the popular jargon, turned me on.

As I became more obsessed with eye-color research and continued to talk and write on the subject, I learned another secret about the advantages of a healthy obsession. In time, people identify you with the obsession and they help to feed it. As I became more and more known as "that eye-color guy," I found that people were going out of their way to send me clippings, references, ideas and observations, suggestions—anything at all that had to do with eye color. My chances to see new relationships and have creative insights were enhanced by all of the extra information that people willingly, cheerfully, freely passed along to me.

Thinking about these experiences, I realized that I, too, responded to the obsessions of others. A nephew is obsessed with major league baseball—I send him clippings from time to time, invite him to ball games, and so forth. A friend is obsessed with organic gardening; I pass on any information I happen to read or hear on the subject. A colleague is interested in therapeutic techniques for reducing anxiety; I give him the benefit of my thinking and reading on the subject. These people are

1. See, for instance, *Newsweek,* Science Section, November 19, 1973.

getting free and unsolicited help from me because it is satisfying to pass on something that I *know* they will be interested in; the more intense the person's interest or obsession, the more likely I am to take time to support it. Of course, a person may have more than one continuing obsession, and we can respond to more than one, but if the person's interests and concerns are too diverse, we fail to identify him with anything and never find occasion to give unsolicited support.

A question you might ask yourself at this point is how you are identified in other people's minds. Is there an obsession or two that you have allowed some healthy growth? It does not have to be something grand or glorious. If you are viewed as a person who loves to cook, people will give you recipes, tips, ideas, enjoy talking with you about food and will enhance your chances of becoming a creative cook. We are not speaking here of just science, invention, art—even though those are important fields of creativity. We are speaking of how anyone, you in particular, can live a more creative life.

Habits of healthy obsession are learned and can be fostered. A basic truth, however, is that one cannot make himself obsessed about something in which he is not freely and genuinely interested. For that reason we cannot and should not try to *work* ourselves into any particular obsession. We can, however, monitor our own thoughts and daydreams to determine what areas of interest just naturally turn us on. Not all of these "recurring themes" are potentials for development. Some are morbid or escapist in nature and do not contain the seeds of a healthy obsession. Other preoccupations are worth nurturing and need only to be allowed to grow from passive interest to active, productive, healthy, creative obsessions. Allow yourself to think more about the productive things you *want* to do and less about the things you *have* to do. That will set the process in motion.

Aha! Thinking

Our obsessions prepare us for creative thought, but there is another necessary element, if our thinking is to be truly creative and not just an accumulation of more and more facts. We must be able to fit the facts together into something which is more than the facts taken alone. We must be able to see relationships, perceive the whole where before we had perceived only the parts, hear a melody where before we had heard only notes. Creativity always involves closing some gap which makes the unknown, known, the unseen, seen. There can never be a chart, a map, a formula for taking that last step. The best we can do, and it is the purpose of this book, is to provide ourselves with experiences in that type of thinking and learn to recognize and appreciate the feeling which goes with it.

I call this crucial step in the creative process, aha! thinking; it has also been called the aha! effect. When we "see" the answer—take the creative step—we are hit with a feeling of aha! The thought which triggers that response is at the heart of the creative process, and it is the capacity for such thoughts that we must increase if we are to grow in our ability to do creative thinking.

Aha! thinking has been cited repeatedly by those who have studied creative output. Progress comes in leaps with a lot of filling in of details in between. These leaps to solutions or new insights come suddenly and trigger the aha! response. The various ways this phenomenon has been described may suggest similar experiences in your own life.

The Aha! Effect has sometimes been called: sudden insight; the Eureka act; a flash of light; illumination. At other times it has been described as: intuitive leap; sudden linkage; closure; revelation; discontinuous progress; rush to solution.

The creative person often describes his or her own experience with such expressions as: "It suddenly dawned on me . . ."

All of us experience aha! thinking from time to time. Creative people are just better prepared, more primed, for this type of thought than others. But how does it happen that some people are more ready for this type of thinking than other people of equal intelligence? Formal education seems not to be the answer; schools traditionally concentrate on teaching incremental learning and reasoning according to rules, which are important skills also, but very different from insightful problem-solving with its sudden leap to a solution. I confess that I do not know how this way of thinking—aha! thinking—is best learned, and there are probably many experiences in one's life that can contribute to that ability. For myself, I am sure that my military experience some fifteen years ago strengthened this type of thinking. As an analyst in an intelligence unit, I often had the game-like challenge of drawing inferences, forming con-clusions, making guesses based on scanty, incomplete information. Trying to see relationships and patterns, trying to match one fact with some other seemingly unrelated fact in that setting served, I believe, as good practice for doing the same thing now. My work now is with psychological data rather than intelligence data, but still I must try to see relationships and try to *match* seemingly unrelated facts that will *fit* into a meaningful theory.

The aspect of my intelligence work I remember best is the fun of the challenge, the game-like quality of what I did. I am convinced that no experience will strengthen aha! thinking unless the person is able to treat the experience as fun, a challenge, a game, a time to play. This playful attitude toward work has been noted repeatedly in the lives of creative people. Repeatedly, these people refer to their creative solutions and breakthroughs and preliminary work involved as a game or a puzzle. This fact, it seems to me, indicates that one way to increase creative or aha! thinking is to *play* with puzzles that are fun to do and that are solved by *sudden* insights.

The Aha! Puzzles

I first became interested in aha! thinking ten years ago while a graduate student at the University of Florida. Part of the graffiti in the men's room of the psychology building was a cryptic formula someone had written in large letters on the wall. I was intrigued by this little puzzle and, of course, had occasion to be reminded of it from time to time. Finally, one day, the answer (yes, obscene) suddenly came to me. It happened that I was studying creativity at the time and I realized that my response to solving the graffiti puzzle was very like the "aha! effect" about which I had been reading. It occurred to me that word puzzles, like the one I had solved, if constructed with certain principles in mind, could serve to test and stimulate aha! thinking. I constructed a test (the Formula

Analysis Test which is included in this book) of items similar in principle to the one I had found on the rest room wall. I tested hundreds of people—high school students, college students, peace corps volunteers, and college faculty members. I found that scores on the test were not correlated significantly with I.Q. scores, but they highly correlated with scores on the best-validated tests of creative thinking. The most satisfying aspect of this experience was that many people who took the test found it fun and wanted to know if I had similar tests that they could take. That led me to believe that test-like puzzles, constructed with the aha! effect in mind, would be an easy, painless, fun way for people to sharpen their creative wits. Over the years I have written numerous puzzles with that purpose in mind and used them in classes and workshops. Those puzzles that people enjoyed I kept, added to, and it is those puzzles that are presented as exercise material in this book. All of them require aha! thinking to some degree and also are meant to be fun. If, as the puzzles are worked, an occasional "aha!" escapes your lips, you will know that the puzzles are serving their intended purpose.

If you have trouble with a particular item and then finally get it, try to analyze why you were initially blocked. In that way, you may detect recurring patterns in your problem-solving behavior that are blocking flexible thinking. For instance, you may find that you are quick to get a strong "set" and then have trouble giving it up when it does not work. On subsequent puzzles you should consciously try to avoid getting locked into any strong set. Or you may find that you have trouble because you are quickly frustrated when you cannot get the answer. If that is the case, you are probably trying too hard and working rather than playing. Ease up, and try to approach the puzzles with a more playful attitude. By monitoring yourself in this way you can identify and endeavor to eliminate any blocking tendencies that may lower your capacity for creative thought. A short introduction is given prior to each type of puzzle which will help you see the ways in which that particular type of puzzle requires flexible thinking. As you attempt the puzzles, keep two things in mind: (1) view the puzzles as a challenge and approach them in a playful mood; and (2) use the puzzles as a way to become more aware of your own approach to situations that require flexible thinking.

In writing the puzzles several criteria were adhered to:

(1) None of the puzzles requires special information or a large vocabulary. In almost every case, you will find that you already know everything you need to know to solve the puzzle. You will need only to "see the solution."

(2) The puzzles are not solved by any step-by-step process. Difficult items are solved by sudden insight—the aha! effect.

(3) Each puzzle is relatively easy in that it is short and contains few items. The advantage of this is that a person can work a complete puzzle at one sitting, even if he or she has only a short time to devote to it. One student kept the puzzles by his bed and worked one each night before going to sleep. A woman kept them in her purse to work on when having to wait at a restaurant or at the beauty shop. Having short puzzles cuts down on the "scanning" time required and makes possible more aha! experiences in a given period of time. Even though the puzzles are short,

you may find some of the items rather difficult. Most people do. All of the items are easy *after you "see" the answer.*

A Final Preliminary Word

Start by trying the Formula Analysis Test and come back to it from time to time until you have solved all of the items. Other than that, it does not matter which puzzles are done in what order. Skip around. Do the ones you find easy or enjoy doing. Be aware of your own thinking process and try to improve your ability to think in a flexible manner. Learn, for yourself, to increase the joy which comes from a sudden "aha!"

The Formula Analysis Test

This is the test mentioned earlier. There are twenty-seven items. Validity studies indicate that this is not a test of intelligence, but it is a test of at least one kind of creative or flexible thinking. Do not be discouraged if you have trouble with the test; most people get fewer than half of the items on their initial try. Answer the ones you can and then stop. Try to remember the unsolved items and come back to the test from time to time and try to solve the items you have not yet solved. Answers may come to you at unexpected times. Many people have reported an answer suddenly occurring to them at times when they were relaxed and not consciously thinking about the test—such as while taking a shower or just prior to falling asleep. This experience, sudden and often unexpected, can give one an idea of why people sometimes talk of their creative insights as though they came from the unconscious mind or some unknown source.

To encourage you to follow the procedure I suggested (i.e., coming back to the test from time to time until you get all the items), I am lowering your temptation to do otherwise by not giving the answers. Except for this test, all answers are given in the back of the book. Take it as a challenge to get all twenty-seven items, on your own, sooner or later.

Instructions: Below are 27 formulas or statements that are to be solved. Write in the blank provided the word or words represented by the underlined part of the formula.

Examples: (1) 3F. = 1 yard (3 <u>feet</u> = 1 yard) (2) 4L.C. = G. L. (4-leaf clover = <u>Good Luck</u>)

Formula Analysis Test—Revised Form

1. M. + M. + N.H. + V.
   + C. + R.I. = <u>N.E.</u>   (1) _____
2. "1B. in the H. = 2 in
   the <u>B</u>."   (2) _____
3. 8D. − 24H. = 1 <u>W</u>.   (3) _____
4. H.H. & M.H. at 12 = <u>N</u>. or
   <u>M</u>.   (4) _____
5. 3 <u>P</u>. = 6   (5) _____
6. 4 J. + 4 Q. + 4 K. =
   all the <u>F.C.</u>   (6) _____
7. S. & M. & T. & W. & T.
   & F. & S. are <u>D. of W</u>.   (7) _____
8. A. + N. + A.F. + M.C.
   + C.G. = <u>A. F.</u>   (8) _____
9. T. = <u>L.S.</u> State   (9) _____
10. 23 Y. − 3 Y. = <u>2D</u>.   (10) _____
11. E. − 8 = <u>Z</u>.   (11) _____
12. 8 P. = 1 <u>G</u>.   (12) _____
13. C. + 6 D. = <u>N.Y.E.</u>   (13) _____
14. <u>S. R.</u> of N. = 3   (14) _____
15. A. & E. were in the <u>G. of
    E</u>.   (15) _____
16. My F. L. & South P. are
    both <u>M.C.</u>   (16) _____
17. "N. N. = <u>G. N.</u>"   (17) _____
18. N. + P. + S. M. =
    <u>S. of C</u>.   (18) _____

19. $1 + 6\,Z. = 1\,\underline{M}.$ (19) _____

20.   B. or G. – F. – M. = O   (20) _____

21.   "R. = R. = $\underline{R}$."   (21) _____

22.   A. L. & J. G. & W. M. &
      J. K. were all $\underline{A}$.   (22) _____

23.   N. + V. + P. + A. +
      A. + C. + P. + I.
      = $\underline{P.\ of\ S}$.   (23) _____

24.   S. + H. of R. = $\underline{U.S.C}$.   (24) _____

25.   P. & N. & D. & Q. & H.D.
      are all $\underline{C}$.   (25) _____

26.   Y. – S. – S. – A. = $\underline{W}$.   (26) _____

27.   Y. + 2 D. = $\underline{T}$.   (27) _____

Embedded
Words
Puzzles

These puzzles, like most of the puzzles in the book, are in a matching format. Matching requires that we find something that will "fit." This searching for something that will match—trying to fit disparate parts together—is a common activity in creative work and for that reason, a matching format is ideal for providing practice in aha! thinking.

The Embedded Words Puzzles help to illustrate one form of blocking that often occurs. Answers that are embedded within other meaningful wholes (in this case words within words) are harder to recognize than when standing alone. The problem is that our recognition of one function may blind us to other functions that could be served by the same elements. This blocking is called "functional fixedness" and is sometimes illustrated by having people solve a problem requiring a box, nails, string, etc. If the box is presented empty, people tend to do well on the problem; if the nails are in the box when the items are presented, many people do poorly because they fail to see the box as useful in solving the problem because it is already serving a function—holding the nails.

Embedded words are similar in concept to embedded pictures which all of us have seen as puzzles in newspapers and magazines. We may have a difficult time seeing the "hidden dog in the tree" or whatever, but once we see it, it is obvious—we cannot not see it from then on. Such is the nature of aha! experiences. But why couldn't we see it earlier? Part of the reason was that the dog's leg functioned as a tree limb, its nose as part of a leaf, and so forth. Like the example above of the box problem we were blocked by "functional fixedness." The problems of embedded answers and functional fixedness in blocking flexible thinking have been extensively demonstrated by psychological studies. Practice with problems of embeddedness is given in these puzzles, and in the next group of puzzles as well. There are four of these puzzles. *Instructions:* Each of the words on the right has at least two shorter words that are embedded in the longer word. To illustrate what is meant by embedded, the word "tart" contains the shorter words "tar" and "art." To solve each item, find two embedded words that, taken together, mean the same thing as one of the words or phrases on the left.

To the left of each item (1, 2, 3, 4 or 5), write, in the space provided, the letter of the correct answer (A, B, C, D or E) and the two embedded words that comprise the answer. Answers to the following puzzles begin on page 97.

Embedded Words Puzzles

Number 1

_____ 1.	Question everyone	A.	Tooling
_____ 2.	Capable devil	B.	Running
_____ 3.	Quarrel	C.	Demon-strable
_____ 4.	Something all members of my family have in common	D.	Basketball
_____ 5.	Not enough out	E.	Tournament

Number 2

_____ 1.	Take Theodore out of the game	A.	Spotlight
_____ 2.	Every pain	B.	Arrested
_____ 3.	Story for pre-Easter	C.	Household
_____ 4.	Notice grass	D.	Teacher
_____ 5.	Children's request to be hugged	E.	Talented

Number 3

_____ 1.	Unhappy insect	A.	Pitching
_____ 2.	Appropriate bright color	B.	Captured
_____ 3.	Tiny tail	C.	Patriotic
_____ 4.	Something acne may do	D.	Weekend
_____ 5.	Attending disturbance	E.	Disadvan-tage

Number 4

_____ 1. Consume almost a dozen   A. Broadest

_____ 2. Royal Family   B. Threatening

_____ 3. Fool Kenneth   C. Handshaking

_____ 4. Billboard   D. Turntable

_____ 5. Price of vase   E. Stricken

Flexibility
Puzzles

These puzzles have been the most popular of any I have used in training sessions. To enjoy them, though, one certainly needs to have a sense of the ridiculous. The puzzles are in a matching format, and some items are matched on the basis of some word or phrase that can have a double meaning. The difficulty in solving these items comes from a mental set which assumes the obvious, but wrong, meaning of the word or phrase. Learning to overcome wrong mental sets is a key factor in learning to think in a flexible and creative manner.

In other items, a correct match depends on seeing that the answer is embedded in some way or other. Since an item may or may not involve embeddedness, more flexibility is required than with the previous puzzles. Another feature which calls for greater flexibility in these puzzles is that embeddedness when present, may be in the words on the left side as well as on the right side. There are 100 of these puzzles.

Instructions: The items in these puzzles are matched on the basis of similar or related meanings. However, the relevant meaning may be disguised in such a way that the connection is not immediately obvious. One type of disguise involves words that have more than one common meaning. Another type of disguise involves words or parts of words that are embedded in longer words. The part of each match that is disguised may be on the left, or it may be on the right.

These puzzles require flexibility and a well-developed sense of the ridiculous. Do not take them too seriously and you will quickly improve at seeing the relationships. Flexibility puzzles answers begin on page 99.

Flexibility Puzzles

Number 1

____ 1. Budget

____ 2. Manifold

____ 3. Noah's creation

____ 4. Filling (and) the bill

____ 5. Far-sighted surgeon

A. Long distance operator

B. Two things obtained from dentist

C. Pick a rose early

D. May be grand-father

E. Newark

Number 2

____ 1. Ground hog

____ 2. Peer group

____ 3. Historian

____ 4. Locomotive

____ 5. Forgive and forget

A. Spectators

B. Past master

C. Draw names at Christmas time

D. Sausage

E. Calls for plea of insanity

Number 3

____ 1. Bulldozer training

____ 2. I share

____ 3. Back burners

____ 4. Marksmanship

A. Rearrange

B. Comes from small bell

C. Grade school

D. Bugs Bunny

_____ 5.   Weeding   E.   Gives tattoo
                                   where it
                                   won't show

Number 4

_____ 1.   Sea trip   A.   Half a debate
_____ 2.   Defective cards   B.   Embarrassing
                                   tear
_____ 3.   Proportion   C.   Early winter
_____ 4.   Fill silo with   D.   Pouring rain
           wheat
_____ 5.   Fall short   E.   Unsuited

Number 5

_____ 1.   Attach   A.   For mice
_____ 2.   Cereal bowl   B.   Give black
                                   eye
_____ 3.   Nymph   C.   Brandish
_____ 4.   Box lid   D.   Pinto
_____ 5.   Freeze   E.   Very few in
                                   Manhattan
                                   traffic

Number 6

_____ 1.   Make up the   A.   Allied
           difference
_____ 2.   George Washington B.   Crooked
                                   umpire
_____ 3.   Outrigger   C.   On the buck-
                                   head

____ 4. Al Smith said he
         would be elected
         president

D. Providence
    attorney

____ 5. Ride fender

E. Pale and color-
    ful faces

Number 7

____ 1. Second hand

A. International
    date line

____ 2. String bass

B. Skip lace

____ 3. Myself

C. Keep your
    catch

____ 4. "I've never told a
         girl this before"

D. Very brief
    applause

____ 5. Snowy slope

E. Theme

Number 8

____ 1. Double deck

A. Recipient of
    foreign aid

____ 2. Being too truthful

B. Underlying

____ 3. Develop self-
         discipline

C. Knock down
    twin

____ 4. Caretaker

D. Whippoorwill

____ 5. Parable

E. Needs no
    handicap

Number 9

____ 1. Scowl

A. Southeast-
    ern bird

____ 2. Bump into dog

B. Poorly made
    goods

____3.	At ease	C.	Ramp up
____4.	Breakfast products	D.	Insulate a wire
____5.	Cover charge	E.	One who kids around

Number 10

____1.	Speak well	A.	Doesn't be-long to us
____2.	Listless	B.	Skit angle
____3.	Results in fall	C.	Buying on impulse
____4.	No tours	D.	Pentagon staff meeting
____5.	General Assembly	E.	Remarkably

Number 11

____1.	Hands	A.	Act of care-less starter
____2.	Gunrunner	B.	Going loves
____3.	Pass time	C.	Totally
____4.	To count up	D.	Hunt soil
____5.	Wildcat driller	E.	When you can't score running

Number 12

____1.	Take the lead	A.	West art
____2.	Rabbi tears	B.	Cat chair
____3.	Parents	C.	Steal metal

_____ 4. Miss the ball

D. Are long and
listen for
dogs

_____ 5. Let us begin

E. We don't own
a home

Number 13

_____ 1. Took

A. Short silence

_____ 2. McKinley speak

B. Little Red
Riding Hood

_____ 3. Minimum

C. Households

_____ 4. Small Russian on
front of car

D. To approve

_____ 5. Foundation

E. Highest in
North
America

Number 14

_____ 1. Baby carriage

A. War plane

_____ 2. Set own

B. Impend

_____ 3. Shift allegiance

C. Jacksonville

_____ 4. Put bend in trail

D. Part for small
typewriter

_____ 5. Pointed tail

E. Wear only
dresses that
hang straight

Number 15

_____ 1. Remove

A. Halfback

_____ 2. No test open

B. Affectionate
people

_____ 3. Gouge leg   C. Shindig
_____ 4. Neck and neck race   D. Letters to
                                            write
_____ 5. Support   E. Cheat at
          indifferently   checkers

Number 16

_____ 1. Roosters' gaze   A. Command to
                                            retreat
_____ 2. Gardener's fear   B. Athens
_____ 3. Moment for making   C. Cadillac's
          amends   price and
                                            prestige
_____ 4. Back order   D. At one time
_____ 5. Old Slacks   E. May beige
                                            tweeds

Number 17

_____ 1. Search Harold   A. Baseball
          for weapon
_____ 2. Air Force dance   B. No heavier
_____ 3. Change tires   C. Almost a
                                            dozen
                                            flippers
_____ 4. A slight   D. Half risk
_____ 5. Tense alarms   E. Progress is
                                            fatiguing

Number 18

_____ 1. To narrow   A. Wagon
_____ 2. Two   B. Would require

a very
large bow

_____ 3. Worry   C. One and the
                                      same

_____ 4. Stay happy, pup   D. Makes the
                                      headlines

_____ 5. Madrid   E. Cure insanity

Number 19

_____ 1. Abdomen   A. Custom built
_____ 2. Cooking   B. Can't get
                                      across
                                      river

_____ 3. Traditional   C. Chief dove
_____ 4. Lie down   D. Naval base
_____ 5. Nob Ridge   E. Change planes

Number 20

_____ 1. Mildred   A. Pulls in lips
_____ 2. Breakthrough   B. Pink
_____ 3. Quick change artist   C. On brief
                                      diet

_____ 4. Stop spout   D. Time to go
                                      back to work

_____ 5. Leaning slightly   E. Pickpocket

Number 21

_____ 1. Rent the penthouse   A. Self-doubt
_____ 2. Priest who hears   B. Curlers
         confessions
_____ 3. Run along   C. To please

_____ 4.   Amiable

D.   To win office in Louisiana

_____ 5.   Fortresses

E.   Director of admissions

Number 22

_____ 1.   Rollins

A.   Hollywood

_____ 2.   Wooden steps

B.   Goat

_____ 3.   Test-tube babies

C.   Lucky basketball shots

_____ 4.   Start own

D.   First airs

_____ 5.   Approach

E.   Alabama

Number 23

_____ 1.   Enlarges hen pen

A.   Wear elevated shoes

_____ 2.   Passport

B.   Double scoop

_____ 3.   Right

C.   Share wine

_____ 4.   Falling star

D.   Doesn't taste like rye

_____ 5.   Cotton gin

E.   Champion skydiver

Number 24

_____ 1.   Fold corners

A.   Coast Guard

_____ 2.   Unable to mimic

B.   Race track window

_____ 3.   Once anxious

C.   In the past tense

_____ 4. Emergency brakes   D. For bashful
                                  sheep

_____ 5. Be there   E. Can tape

Number 25

_____ 1. Vice lord   A. Very cheap
                                  surgery

_____ 2. Coin operated   B. Overbearing
                                  parents

_____ 3. Snake highway   C. To get from
                                  Houston to
                                  New York

_____ 4. Population problem   D. Board
_____ 5. Gone   E. Sinking

Number 26

_____ 1. Hijack   A. Make score
_____ 2. Land office   B. Song of
                                  support

_____ 3. Fortune   C. Buckboard
_____ 4. Eating an apple   D. What not to
                                  say to
                                  the ripper

_____ 5. The Federal Reserve   E. Be elected

Number 27

_____ 1. Exile monarch   A. Soap dishes
_____ 2. Peace   B. Highway
                                  patrolman

_____ 3.   Speed reader   C.   Banking

_____ 4.   Barracks   D.   Land given
                                      by Spanish
                                      king

_____ 5.   Flagrant   E.   Star perform-
                                      er in physical
                                      education

Number 28

_____ 1.   Outgrowth   A.   For a Navy
                                      career, girls

_____ 2.   Joint he waves   B.   Linebacker

_____ 3.   Alias   C.   Bayonet
                                      practice

_____ 4.   Slow ticket salesman D.   Like the
                                      heavy-weight
                                      boxer

_____ 5.   Cut classes   E.   Double play

Number 29

_____ 1.   Noel Coward   A.   False arrest

_____ 2.   Lumber company   B.   Drunks taking
                                      a walk

_____ 3.   Misapprehension   C.   Attempt it,
                                      Edgar

_____ 4.   Poetry   D.   Child afraid
                                      of Santa

_____ 5.   Alaskan urban area   E.   Metronome

Number 30

_____ 1.   Box in ground   A.   No cover
charge

_____ 2.   Proofread   B.   Cuff links

_____ 3.   Committed to the   C.   Look at
local electorate   photograph

_____ 4.   Fine for public   D.   Starts with
nudity   a bell

_____ 5.   Hit chain   E.   Homeward
bound

Number 31

_____ 1.   Detectives' dance   A.   Carrot

_____ 2.   Holding company   B.   Cease being
mad

_____ 3.   Endanger   C.   Refusing to
say good-bye

_____ 4.   Earn loathing   D.   Private
eyeball

_____ 5.   Rust   E.   Wind is
gust

Number 32

_____ 1.   Better half   A.   Ankle

_____ 2.   Drill Sergeant   B.   Light switch

_____ 3.   Bloodshot   C.   Score above
average

_____ 4.   For mild punishment   D.   Is passionate

_____ 5. Legend   E. Private
                                        tutor

Number 33

_____ 1. Get uptight   A. Notice cream
_____ 2. Evaluate Russian plane   B. Minute store
                                        ad
_____ 3. Ice milk   C. Migrate
_____ 4. Short time for book   D. Fail to sleep
                                        it off
_____ 5. Blackboard   E. Remarkable

Number 34

_____ 1. Take turns   A. Cry improperly
_____ 2. Not so bright   B. Begin
                                        overeating
_____ 3. A wee kiss even   C. Scarcities
_____ 4. Tear up urban areas   D. Days
_____ 5. Start again   E. Steal part of
                                        a race track

Number 35

_____ 1. A red we trust   A. True to life
_____ 2. Job change for mag-   B. Cross English
          azine writer   Channel
_____ 3. Sunlit   C. Put an end to
_____ 4. Sit on   D. May be found
                                        on old
                                        submarines
_____ 5. Oppose the BBC   E. Rayon

Number 36

_____ 1. Go motoring   A. Looks at mine
_____ 2. Date palm   B. Bump heads
_____ 3. Ramparts   C. Drive stake
_____ 4. Eyesore   D. Worthy of
                                    notice
_____ 5. Not able   E. Where to put
                                    the flowers
                                    or candy

Number 37

_____ 1. Double header   A. Ski dangle
_____ 2. Nagging wife   B. Crooked coin
_____ 3. Skip practice   C. Manager
_____ 4. Auto accident   D. King ranch
          information
_____ 5. Widespread   E. Requires a
                                    rope

Number 38

_____ 1. Cart rails   A. Malinger
_____ 2. Increase in amount   B. Fly by night
          of military service
_____ 3. Stay, Mom   C. Roads
_____ 4. From bet systems   D. Hitchhike
_____ 5. June 21   E. Design of
                                    our flag

Number 39

_____ 1. Get ready to drive   A. Teddy bear

_____ 2.   Repair

_____ 3.   Oriental customs agents

_____ 4.   Totally

_____ 5.   Drum major

B.   Narrow academic specialty

C.   Chinese checkers

D.   Settee

E.   Marry again

Number 40

_____ 1.   Quick look around

_____ 2.   Adjust

_____ 3.   Must stay in base path

_____ 4.   Coincide

_____ 5.   Shamrock

A.   Killing money

B.   Slide rule

C.   Fair commercial

D.   Imitation diamond

E.   Briefcase

Number 41

_____ 1.   Fellow gangster

_____ 2.   Spouse

_____ 3.   Buys large sizes and a basketball

_____ 4.   Typewriter

_____ 5.   Elegant breathing

A.   Shopping center

B.   Fancy pants

C.   Brotherhood

D.   Hum animated

E.   Novelist

Number 42

_____ 1.   Correspondence

_____ 2.   Hurt Roosevelt

_____ 3.   Must ache

_____ 4.   Shell shock

A.   Pawn ammunition

B.   Trading post

C.   Habit

D.   Painted

___ 5. Small joke

E. Tickles the
one kissed

Number 43

___ 1. Begin crease

A. Amount

___ 2. Office hours

B. Hockey player's
leisure time

___ 3. Horse

C. Batter whipped

___ 4. Excessive use of
articles

D. Plea for more

___ 5. Struck out

E. Atheism

Number 44

___ 1. Pocket change

A. Echo

___ 2. Resound

B. Alteration of
pool table

___ 3. Life raft

C. Listen to
storm

___ 4. A ship

D. Overpopulated

___ 5. Hearth under

E. Enter sports

Number 45

___ 1. Big buddy

A. Kennel fee

___ 2. A bad tool

B. Good medicine

___ 3. Topsail

C. Hitch Alice

___ 4. Strike cup

D. Fatally

___ 5. Current

E. Bump liars

Number 46

___ 1. Impact

A. Trouble
shooter

_____ 2. Cement mixer

_____ 3. Expensive wife

_____ 4. Ask questions at a duel

_____ 5. Tangent

B. Furl over

C. Male lifeguard

D. Repair kitchen utensil

E. Naughty deed

Number 47

_____ 1. Subdivision

_____ 2. Peanut butter

_____ 3. Boys have

_____ 4. Relatives look on

_____ 5. Idea laces

A. King ape

B. Defuzzing

C. Purpose of depth charge

D. I'll give you good cards

E. Undersized goat

Number 48

_____ 1. Combination lock

_____ 2. We teach one

_____ 3. Thermal underwear

_____ 4. Call your shot

_____ 5. Small cloth or paper

A. Short shot

B. Kidnap kin

C. Pickpocket

D. To put out matches

E. Part wig and part natural

Number 49

_____ 1. Continue

_____ 2. Melting pot

_____ 3. They are dwarfs or fairies

A. Themselves

B. Goon

C. Exercising

____ 4. Bet ray   D. Seat belts
____ 5. Spanking   E. Deceive

Number 50

____ 1. Advanced standing   A. For tiny
                                            servings
____ 2. Printing press   B. Bowstring
____ 3. Genial president   C. Walked
____ 4. Last thing pulled   D. Crowded first
         in puppet show   grade
____ 5. Weep late   E. War mike

Number 51

____ 1. Wastebasket   A. Gets even
____ 2. Trigger revolt   B. Fetch the
                                            girl
____ 3. Score touchdown   C. Buck Rogers
         and extra point
____ 4. Cart Agnew   D. Make shot after
                                            buzzer
____ 5. Go together   E. Shiny license
                                            plate

Number 52

____ 1. Thinking   A. Beware of
                                            blowout
____ 2. Not read   B. Barroom
____ 3. Superior court   C. Lessons
____ 4. Save electricity   D. Skinny monarch
____ 5. Lawyer's office   E. Woo the boss

Number 53

___ 1.	Moll	A.	Decimate
___ 2.	Footboard	B.	Sell sporting goods
___ 3.	I'll marry about Christmas	C.	Amen corner
___ 4.	Ballads	D.	Ski
___ 5.	One girl getting all the dates	E.	Girlhood

Number 54

___ 1.	Underground	A.	Tomatoes
___ 2.	Send message to officials	B.	A donation
___ 3.	An active people	C.	Cheap coffee
___ 4.	Dresses went in old days	D.	Wire wheels
___ 5.	Noise of a boy	E.	Aladdin

Number 55

___ 1.	Rock music	A.	Birds
___ 2.	Take charge	B.	Lullaby
___ 3.	Beacon man	C.	Coaching
___ 4.	Cat skill	D.	Taxi fare
___ 5.	Having sympathy	E.	Learn to swindle

Number 56

___ 1.	Doctor's house	A.	Dartmouth
___ 2.	Landmark	B.	Clothes on line

_____ 3. Manila folder   C. Oriental
                                   lawn chair

_____ 4. Sundries   D. Tire track on
                                   runway

_____ 5. Sharp tongued   E. Changes
                                   residence

Number 57

_____ 1. Stitch   A. Ticker tape
_____ 2. Office of the boss   B. Hemlock
_____ 3. Growing apart   C. Fireplace
_____ 4. Mends broken heart? D. Missing links
_____ 5. Very bad golf shot   E. Balding

Number 58

_____ 1. A girl yearns   A. Kindred
_____ 2. The fatted calf   B. Follows a
                                   drought
_____ 3. Asphalt   C. Sign of the
                                   bicycle rider
_____ 4. Compassionate   D. Form ink
          comrade
_____ 5. Be strain   E. Snake stop

Number 59

_____ 1. Draw poker   A. Slow Susan
_____ 2. Don't betray   B. Dead gun-
          country   fighter
_____ 3. Preside as judge   C. Not reason
_____ 4. The last issue   D. Treadmill
_____ 5. Recapping shop   E. Workbench

Number 60

____ 1.	Alternatives	A.	Perpetual motion
____ 2.	New Orleans rock	B.	Last one
____ 3.	Aim of filibuster	C.	Trade winds
____ 4.	V for Victory	D.	Missionary's job
____ 5.	Tend to my watch and I'll tend to yours	E.	Roman basket-ball team

Number 61

____ 1.	Lagoon	A.	West Coast thug
____ 2.	Mushroom	B.	Missing
____ 3.	Truck like	C.	Blank check
____ 4.	Be off key	D.	Vanish
____ 5.	Examination for amnesia	E.	Space for sled dogs to run

Number 62

____ 1.	Tom	A.	Chain of command
____ 2.	Sweet roll	B.	Head start
____ 3.	Cabbage sprout	C.	Loaded dice
____ 4.	Power lines	D.	Visiting
____ 5.	Not a town house	E.	Cat's paw

Number 63

____ 1.	Typesetter	A.	Information please

_____ 2. Booking   B. Trade cars

_____ 3. A drill sergeant   C. Irish
      doesn't say

_____ 4. Crowded fishing   D. Streamlined

_____ 5. Makeshift   E. Did I scare
      you, Sire?

Number 64

_____ 1. Out of bounds   A. Wanton

_____ 2. Have a double   B. Untied

_____ 3. Wish to board   C. Now acknowl-
      edge

_____ 4. Ignorant of women   D. Bet win
      soldiers

_____ 5. Sports car   E. Show off old
      injury

Number 65

_____ 1. Decade   A. Job for press
      agent

_____ 2. Have no bearing   B. Bargains

_____ 3. Start out   C. Conclusive
      evidence

_____ 4. Nonprofit organizations   D. Christmas
      drink

_____ 5. Soundproof   E. Faulty skates

Number 66

_____ 1. Size up   A. Wearing
      hospital
      gown

_____ 2.   Pleasure   B.   Pleases fairy
                                      godmother

_____ 3.   Ill suited   C.   Gain weight

_____ 4.   Wishing well   D.   Isolate

_____ 5.   I'm so tardy   E.   Ask confidently

Number 67

_____ 1.   Understand   A.   Well made

_____ 2.   Shortcoming   B.   Line coach

_____ 3.   Holds cue cards   C.   Kids at birth-
                                      day party

_____ 4.   Cured   D.   Slouch

_____ 5.   Tailspin   E.   Rotting
                                      insulation

Number 68

_____ 1.   Pull with wrecker   A.   In prison
                                      choir

_____ 2.   Slaphappy   B.   To wit

_____ 3.   Grand slam   C.   Mistreat a
                                      dwarf

_____ 4.   Accost   D.   Angry exit

_____ 5.   Striped bass   E.   Electricity
                                      bill

Number 69

_____ 1.   Fall through   A.   Unlike

_____ 2.   Got oil   B.   Brief greeting

_____ 3.   Short wave   C.   Make a tempor-
                                      ary barnyard
                                      repair

____ 4. League of Nations   D. Start work
____ 5. Propagate   E. December 21

Number 70

____ 1. Who not to loan   A. Light sockets
         soap to
____ 2. Medieval hero   B. Stark night
____ 3. Sound better   C. Barkeeper
____ 4. Pickpocket   D. Needed by gui-
                                       tar player
____ 5. Frail knees and   E. Plays the odds
         elbows

Number 71

____ 1. Divorce   A. Complete stop
____ 2. Snapshot   B. We drift
____ 3. Roofer   C. Trouble with
                                       shorts just
                                       out of dryer
____ 4. Tend to fumble   D. Leave a mess
____ 5. Poor furlough   E. Greenbacks

Number 72

____ 1. Dear Santa Claus   A. Nylon gears
____ 2. Gothic cups   B. Bearing
____ 3. Circle up   C. Represents
____ 4. A Brooklyn rabbit   D. Dawn
____ 5. Fir stray   E. Drink water
                                       for cure

Number 73

____ 1.	Fire department	A.	Strict diet
____ 2.	None sold	B.	Top ace
____ 3.	Snack bar	C.	Capsize
____ 4.	Walk back and forth	D.	All are young
____ 5.	Toy pistol	E.	Get rid of the whole group

Number 74

____ 1.	Hair mussed up	A.	So what
____ 2.	Bonnet for mother hog	B.	Eye strain
____ 3.	Afraid	C.	Part of Adam's garden
____ 4.	Sweden	D.	Departed
____ 5.	Looks at locomotive	E.	Bombing mission

Number 75

____ 1.	Tastes wine	A.	Top secret
____ 2.	I'm feeling good	B.	Southern bread
____ 3.	Gets a wag	C.	Eat pork
____ 4.	Maximum	D.	Puppet
____ 5.	Scrolls	E.	Amok

Number 76

____ 1.	Beat	A.	Vanished
____ 2.	May have little snakes	B.	Causing girl to go broke

____ 3.	Pull over	C.	Pair of moccasins
____ 4.	Not race	D.	Loss of influence
____ 5.	Break in glass	E.	Attend

Number 77

____ 1.	Fable	A.	Top coat
____ 2.	Cross examination	B.	Capable of flunking
____ 3.	Aircraft	C.	Lighter fluid
____ 4.	Paint that shows	D.	Job for eye doctor
____ 5.	Floats	E.	Announcing

Number 78

____ 1.	Bookmark	A.	South Pole
____ 2.	Widen the street	B.	Fly paper
____ 3.	Justice	C.	Schedule Biblical writer
____ 4.	Mattresses	D.	Chip off the old block
____ 5.	Kite	E.	Get hair wet

Number 79

____ 1.	Fall in grain	A.	Off arms
____ 2.	Fifth Amendment	B.	Drizzle
____ 3.	Included in vehicle tally	C.	Sin gal most
____ 4.	Agricultural	D.	Ponti account

_____ 5. Hum

E. Water down bottle of whiskey

Number 80

_____ 1. Catch at

A. Saying grace

_____ 2. Jet set

B. Roll call

_____ 3. Seven come eleven

C. Persian conversing with Siamese

_____ 4. No tab sent

D. Quick hatch

_____ 5. Name dropping in Monaco

E. Present

Number 81

_____ 1. Out and out

A. Of flight

_____ 2. Monologue

B. Bourbon Street

_____ 3. Parallel bars

C. Solid state

_____ 4. Hashed

D. Double play

_____ 5. Lenient sentence

E. Fun house

Number 82

_____ 1. Snow bank

A. Trust company

_____ 2. Rear view

B. In an atomic nightmare

_____ 3. For altogether

C. She has a good voice

_____ 4. Fall outfits

D. Book by Dr. Spock

_____ 5. Put out the best silver

E. Get loan without collateral

Number 83

____ 1. Fighter plane   A. Whistle
____ 2. Banker   B. Hopefully not
                                    horizontal
____ 3. Refuses   C. Fancy pool
                                    shooter
____ 4. Electrical inspector   D. Circuit judge
____ 5. Bullet   E. Article in
                                    magazine

Number 84

____ 1. Be trigger happy   A. First down
____ 2. Old tub   B. Snarl
____ 3. Paratrooper who for-   C. Ring bearer
         gets chute
____ 4. At angle   D. Inside the
                                    turkey
____ 5. Dressing room   E. When fight
                                    thrown

Number 85

____ 1. After work   A. Swear
____ 2. Break ground   B. Post office
____ 3. Important   C. Fair play
____ 4. Mixed reviews   D. Corral
____ 5. Left one when facing   E. Foreign bug
         northwest

Number 86

____ 1. Cell mate   A. Stern looks
____ 2. Marrow   B. Insects

_____ 3. Eyelashes   C. Give money for
                                            a good cause

_____ 4. Where fanatics   D. Plow sloppily
          congregate

_____ 5. Fundamental hospital   E. Pen pal

Number 87

_____ 1. No strikes   A. Rich uncle

_____ 2. Old Ironsides   B. Settle out
                                            of court

_____ 3. Jumpsuit   C. Hardship

_____ 4. Put on the dog   D. Bow lawfully

_____ 5. Has will power   E. Tease the
                                            pup

Number 88

_____ 1. My taxi   A. Flying tackle

_____ 2. Mild cheese   B. Seepage

_____ 3. For help at Capitol   C. Cabinet

_____ 4. Quick delivery of   D. U.S. Grant
          fishing gear

_____ 5. Foreign aid   E. Results in
                                            faint smile

Number 89

_____ 1. Too much play   A. These

_____ 2. All single births   B. Dodge City

_____ 3. Bug a crooner   C. Not win

_____ 4. Take the by-pass   D. Rubbing the
                                            wrong way

_____ 5. Virginia to Florida   E. Tire skid

Number 90

____ 1.	Example	A.	Strike a match
____ 2.	Manicure	B.	Yellow
____ 3.	Refuse to be married	C.	Baton
____ 4.	How to express pain	D.	No longer enough
____ 5.	Spinning rod	E.	My patient

Number 91

____ 1.	Baronage	A.	Airspace
____ 2.	Just losses	B.	Lipstick
____ 3.	To whiskey	C.	Exclude minors
____ 4.	Wind velocity	D.	Never again
____ 5.	Lockjaw	E.	Purpose of Franklin's kite

Number 92

____ 1.	Nevertheless	A.	Plunder
____ 2.	Leave third	B.	Which piece of pie taken by boy
____ 3.	Our group naughty	C.	Steal away home
____ 4.	Unders	D.	Hold back
____ 5.	Rest rain	E.	Weevil

Number 93

____ 1.	Use hair spray	A.	Bankrupt
____ 2.	Stamp	B.	Set apart

_____ 3.   Second rate   C.   Patron saint
                                            of electricians?

_____ 4.   Ace through ten   D.   Very quick
                                            evaluation

_____ 5.   Allowed   E.   Preface

Number 94

_____ 1.   Checking account   A.   Fast asleep
_____ 2.   Aforesaid   B.   Still life
_____ 3.   Bring up rear   C.   Warns other
                                            golfers

_____ 4.   Easy dieting   D.   Cross
                                            examination

_____ 5.   Stirring and   E.   Raise raise
           drinking

Number 95

_____ 1.   Rugby stands   A.   Power line
_____ 2.   Batting average   B.   Say it
                                            pretty well

_____ 3.   Accord   C.   Daybreak
_____ 4.   State fair   D.   Normal
                                            winking

_____ 5.   Holiday   E.   Artificial
                                            turf

Number 96

_____ 1.   Boxer's strategy   A.   Healthy plant
_____ 2.   Show disapproval at   B.   Wake up!
           opera

_____ 3. Come to order   C. Depressed
                                     drunk
_____ 4. High and low   D. Floor plan
_____ 5. Shoot straight   E. Rock bass

Number 97

_____ 1. Skywriting   A. Reinforce
_____ 2. Far-fetched   B. Suspended
                                     sentence
_____ 3. Extreme egotism   C. Baton
_____ 4. Cavalry   D. Imported
_____ 5. If you don't make   E. If lawless
          any outs

Number 98

_____ 1. Washer woman   A. First batter
_____ 2. Above board   B. Good one
_____ 3. Refuse   C. Lady
                                     plumber
_____ 4. Person stared down   D. Make elec-
                                     trical repair
_____ 5. Finished with baby talk E. Rafter

Number 99

_____ 1. High noon   A. Legal pad
_____ 2. At loose ends   B. Command
_____ 3. Official residence   C. Reappears
_____ 4. Harvest a fruit   D. Where to pass

_____ 5.   Written after Fargo
           or Bismarck

E.   Start drink-
     ing early or
     quit late

Number 100

_____ 1.   Early evening   A.   Stops
_____ 2.   Opposed to painting   B.   Automatically
_____ 3.   Always on our side   C.   Burn car trim
_____ 4.   Pa uses   D.   Quick revenge
_____ 5.   Search Rome   E.   Again start

Anagram
Matching
Puzzles

Most people have done anagrams of one kind or another as a parlor game. When I was growing up, a popular game at Christmas parties was to see who could make the most words by using the letters contained in the word, "Christmas." Similar tasks have been used by psychologists as measures of flexibility and creative fluency. Success on anagram-like tasks has been found to correlate very well with other measures of creative thinking. The anagram puzzles in this book are based on a format somewhat different from the old parlor game. Here, each item has only one right answer.

The previous two puzzles required that a person be able to see a word embedded in some other word. On the Anagram Matching Puzzles, some words have to be completely broken down and the letters rearranged to make another word in order to make an appropriate match. Part of the difficulty, though, is in knowing which words are to be changed since half of the words are in their correct form to start with. These puzzles require that the person be flexible in rearranging the letters to form an anagram and also in knowing when to do so. There are eighty of these puzzles.

Instructions: These puzzles involve matching two words that are closely associated. The association is such that the word on the left is often followed by the word on the right (e.g., home plate, horsepower, etc.). However, in each case, the letters of one or the other (but not both) of the words given must be rearranged to form some other word that can be matched with its associate on the other side. This type of puzzle requires flexibility since a given word may need to be transformed into another word or it may be acceptable as it is. Try this example:

| ____ 1. | See | A. | Walk |
| ____ 2. | Dies | B. | Was |

The answers are 1B, "Seesaw"—the letters in "was" were rearranged to form "saw"; and 2A, "Sidewalk"—the letters in the word "dies" w rearranged to form "side." Note that the word in the pair which needed to be changed was on the right in Item 1B, and on the left in Item 2A. Part of the challenge comes from not knowing ahead of time which words have to be rearranged and which can stay as they are. Answers to Anagram Matching Puzzles begin on page 122.

Anagram Matching Puzzles

Number 1

____ 1.	Sirloin	A.	Claus
____ 2.	Satan	B.	Caned
____ 3.	Balm	C.	Takes
____ 4.	Outer	D.	Chops
____ 5.	Square	E.	Scape

Number 2

____ 1.	Rangoon	A.	Bag
____ 2.	Clark	B.	Beaver
____ 3.	Brag	C.	Bagel
____ 4.	Agree	D.	Tame
____ 5.	Room	E.	Rumba

Number 3

____ 1.	Haves	A.	Peter
____ 2.	Atlantic	B.	Saw
____ 3.	Basal	C.	Canoe
____ 4.	China	D.	Cream
____ 5.	Satin	E.	Wood

Number 4

____ 1.	Nap	A.	Fuzz
____ 2.	Liar	B.	Ohio
____ 3.	Bean	C.	Talks
____ 4.	Koran	D.	Cake
____ 5.	Cheap	E.	Road

Number 5

___ 1.	Pot	A.	Boss
___ 2.	Corn	B.	Snail
___ 3.	Trial	C.	Debar
___ 4.	Brick	D.	Secret
___ 5.	Finger	E.	Moans

Number 6

___ 1.	Beauty	A.	Dean
___ 2.	Rebut	B.	Bubble
___ 3.	Hair	C.	Loans
___ 4.	Paso	D.	Force
___ 5.	Great	E.	Prays

Number 7

___ 1.	Tab	A.	Man
___ 2.	Raced	B.	Cause
___ 3.	Steak	C.	Rapids
___ 4.	Turn	D.	Amen
___ 5.	Nick	E.	Coast

Number 8

___ 1.	Plea	A.	Fear
___ 2.	Blind	B.	Out
___ 3.	Bus	C.	Stead
___ 4.	Heaps	D.	Face
___ 5.	Ice	E.	Steak

Number 9

___ 1.	Earl	A.	Force
___ 2.	Stew	B.	Lube

_____3. First   C. Tear
_____4. Skat   D. Team
_____5. Navy   E. Life

Number 10

_____1. Ski   A. Jerk
_____2. Flood   B. Flier
_____3. Idols   C. Ogled
_____4. Keen   D. Diet
_____5. Air   E. State

Number 11

_____1. Sand   A. Swine
_____2. Grape   B. Spiel
_____3. Sole   C. Sent
_____4. Bird   D. Cart
_____5. Flog   E. Weight

Number 12

_____1. Full   A. Wrong
_____2. Polo   B. Bared
_____3. Blue   C. Alarm
_____4. About   D. Cafe
_____5. Fleas   E. Table

Number 13

_____1. Knead   A. Pleat
_____2. Grad   B. Race
_____3. Gates   C. Coach
_____4. Peaks   D. Eye
_____5. Hot   E. Easy

Number 14

___ 1.	Night	A.	Logan
___ 2.	Peat	B.	Ream
___ 3.	Run	C.	What
___ 4.	Spring	D.	Worm
___ 5.	Salt	E.	Chance

Number 15

___ 1.	Boot	A.	Cried
___ 2.	Seat	B.	Colt
___ 3.	Apple	C.	Traps
___ 4.	Crews	D.	Blest
___ 5.	Blood	E.	Driver

Number 16

___ 1.	Blue	A.	Dirge
___ 2.	Mined	B.	After
___ 3.	Slipped	C.	Skid
___ 4.	Three	D.	Wound
___ 5.	Shelf	E.	Jacket

Number 17

___ 1.	Lime	A.	Rinse
___ 2.	Police	B.	Stone
___ 3.	North	C.	Lope
___ 4.	Class	D.	Point
___ 5.	Stew	E.	Post

Number 18

___ 1.	Stop	A.	Sing
___ 2.	Sink	B.	Stream

____ 3.	Lump	C.	Tree
____ 4.	Tutor	D.	Rated
____ 5.	Tire	E.	Flint

Number 19

____ 1.	Hair	A.	Slate
____ 2.	Bear	B.	Rabid
____ 3.	Lance	C.	Back
____ 4.	Chars	D.	Helmet
____ 5.	Front	E.	Gape

Number 20

____ 1.	Delta	A.	Tapes
____ 2.	Laud	B.	Shift
____ 3.	Air	C.	Cards
____ 4.	Tooth	D.	Penal
____ 5.	Rage	E.	Control

Number 21

____ 1.	Earns	A.	Toga
____ 2.	Hot	B.	East
____ 3.	Billy	C.	Fry
____ 4.	Ink	D.	Saint
____ 5.	Malls	E.	Drum

Number 22

____ 1.	Span	A.	Deeps
____ 2.	Sugar	B.	Shut
____ 3.	Blow	C.	Beset
____ 4.	Full	D.	Screw
____ 5.	Rock	E.	Game

Number 23

____ 1.	Dare	A.	Thrift
____ 2.	Pends	B.	Sheik
____ 3.	Reef	C.	Lived
____ 4.	Nerve	D.	Loader
____ 5.	Hitch	E.	More

Number 24

____ 1.	Live	A.	Eye
____ 2.	Snow	B.	Outer
____ 3.	Mores	C.	Tier
____ 4.	Paper	D.	Bite
____ 5.	Forts	E.	Code

Number 25

____ 1.	Fish	A.	Romp
____ 2.	Spilt	B.	Level
____ 3.	Senior	C.	Based
____ 4.	Glass	D.	Shook
____ 5.	Bares	E.	Toothed

Number 26

____ 1.	Shoe	A.	Graze
____ 2.	Calk	B.	Scale
____ 3.	Out	C.	Scat
____ 4.	Ward	D.	Luster
____ 5.	Star	E.	Back

Number 27

____ 1.	Heads	A.	Preview
____ 2.	Dare	B.	Tree

____3. Grate   C. Leaps
____4. Snake   D. Lakes
____5. Mental   E. Sir

Number 28

____1. Vale   A. Mint
____2. Spare   B. Frat
____3. Life   C. Thaw
____4. Some   D. Eclipse
____5. Orals   E. Cutlet

Number 29

____1. Harps   A. Tree
____2. Lamp   B. Biter
____3. Prat   C. Shooter
____4. Indian   D. Bowl
____5. Death   E. Time

Number 30

____1. Cowboy   A. Rule
____2. Cores   B. Boost
____3. Live   C. Card
____4. Filed   D. Trip
____5. Idles   E. Tocks

Number 31

____1. Slat   A. Warts
____2. Last   B. Mines
____3. Pat   C. Burst
____4. Could   D. Dance
____5. Ice   E. Spick

Number 32

___1.	Buffalo	A.	Smoke
___2.	Tone	B.	Day
___3.	Needs	C.	Shred
___4.	Moods	D.	Walker
___5.	Peels	E.	Book

Number 33

___1.	Fishing	A.	Tree
___2.	Sea	B.	Sport
___3.	Vile	C.	Wire
___4.	Melon	D.	Leer
___5.	Golden	E.	Lure

Number 34

___1.	Evens	A.	Dame
___2.	Heart	B.	Dwarfs
___3.	Mite	C.	Left
___4.	Sun	D.	Bomb
___5.	Tenor	E.	Sire

Number 35

___1.	Baker	A.	Guard
___2.	Tan	B.	Laces
___3.	Wage	C.	Bracelet
___4.	March	D.	Fluid
___5.	Ascot	E.	Hill

Number 36

___1.	Lacks	A.	Valley
___2.	Hated	B.	Angel

_____3. Bicycle   C. Off
_____4. Car   D. Doria
_____5. Right   E. Plead

Number 37

_____1. Chain   A. Dawn
_____2. Edgar   B. Town
_____3. Egg   C. Glean
_____4. Magic   D. School
_____5. Arch   E. Hades

Number 38

_____1. Sad   A. Car
_____2. Aft   B. Back
_____3. Quads   C. Cask
_____4. Steam   D. Syrup
_____5. Ample   E. Hate

Number 39

_____1. Wise   A. Cake
_____2. Macks   B. Up
_____3. Fair   C. Dab
_____4. Weak   D. Shear
_____5. Early   E. Care

Number 40

_____1. Canoe   A. Claps
_____2. Tie   B. While
_____3. Muck   C. Reak
_____4. Lane   D. To
_____5. Mane   E. Perch

Number 41

___ 1.	Window	A.	Nape
___ 2.	Rate	B.	Grinder
___ 3.	Groan	C.	Shade
___ 4.	Palm	D.	Drop
___ 5.	Manor	E.	Empire

Number 42

___ 1.	Pinta	A.	Lick
___ 2.	Waste	B.	Strap
___ 3.	Shams	C.	Gland
___ 4.	Last	D.	Brush
___ 5.	Bear	E.	Hit

Number 43

___ 1.	Oil	A.	Flit
___ 2.	Peon	B.	Door
___ 3.	Nest	C.	Swell
___ 4.	Ski	D.	Number
___ 5.	Grown	E.	Forth

Number 44

___ 1.	Noel	A.	Bush
___ 2.	Ever	B.	Ranger
___ 3.	Sore	C.	Wing
___ 4.	Girth	D.	Rome
___ 5.	Iron	E.	Slung

Number 45

___ 1.	Worth	A.	Pigeon
___ 2.	Lisp	B.	Tacks

____3. Loots   C.   Boast
____4. Life   D.   Back
____5. Smoke   E.   Shod

Number 46

____1. Point   A.   Beans
____2. Tea   B.   Cod
____3. Strait   C.   Decal
____4. Pace   D.   Box
____5. Craig   E.   Snoop

Number 47

____1. Mass   A.   Robe
____2. Name   B.   Place
____3. Draw   C.   Aimed
____4. Ship   D.   Corner
____5. Teak   E.   Phase

Number 48

____1. Horse   A.   Mark
____2. Rated   B.   Files
____3. Diary   C.   Lame
____4. Hater   D.   Farm
____5. Oat   E.   Quake

Number 49

____1. Relay   A.   Bolt
____2. Mates   B.   Face
____3. Vase   C.   Bird
____4. Bath   D.   Bore
____5. Ink   E.   Ship

Number 50

____ 1.	Salve	A.	Nave
____ 2.	Weather	B.	Broth
____ 3.	State	C.	Ship
____ 4.	Trays	D.	Bud
____ 5.	Heart	E.	Cat

Number 51

____ 1.	Ice	A.	Devil
____ 2.	Hocks	B.	Fish
____ 3.	Marine	C.	Crops
____ 4.	Short	D.	Troops
____ 5.	Words	E.	Clod

Number 52

____ 1.	Peptic	A.	Free
____ 2.	Coins	B.	Stud
____ 3.	Cost	C.	Diver
____ 4.	Line	D.	Cruel
____ 5.	Saw	E.	Boom

Number 53

____ 1.	Past	A.	Strings
____ 2.	French	B.	Teens
____ 3.	Slow	C.	Spoke
____ 4.	Home	D.	Fires
____ 5.	Super	E.	Rowen

Number 54

____ 1.	Peek	A.	House
____ 2.	Horse	B.	Tingling

_____ 3. Snipe   C.   Line
_____ 4. Flag   D.   Pore
_____ 5. Jump   E.   Notes

Number 55

_____ 1. Fire   A.   Shill
_____ 2. Rifts   B.   Loop
_____ 3. Beverly   C.   Way
_____ 4. Pills   D.   Wrote
_____ 5. Water   E.   Base

Number 56

_____ 1. Straw   A.   Silt
_____ 2. Thing   B.   Stove
_____ 3. Hoots   C.   Light
_____ 4. Shopping   D.   Table
_____ 5. Runt   E.   Sayer

Number 57

_____ 1. Baker   A.   Corps
_____ 2. Acted   B.   Charm
_____ 3. Forward   C.   Say
_____ 4. Put   D.   Aides
_____ 5. Hare   E.   Down

Number 58

_____ 1. Drum   A.   Bake
_____ 2. Race   B.   Abet
_____ 3. Calm   C.   Proof
_____ 4. Fair   D.   Free
_____ 5. Lake   E.   Dale

Number 59

___1.	Male	A.	Show
___2.	Tale	B.	Skin
___3.	Ship	C.	Duck
___4.	Far	D.	Meat
___5.	Harks	E.	Seat

Number 60

___1.	Nepal	A.	Basket
___2.	Mean	B.	Tree
___3.	Reap	C.	Sake
___4.	Sweat	D.	Truck
___5.	Water	E.	Slags

Number 61

___1.	Sweet	A.	Ranger
___2.	Nip	B.	Earth
___3.	Layer	C.	Up
___4.	Earn	D.	By
___5.	Taxes	E.	Switch

Number 62

___1.	Hear	A.	Scuff
___2.	Wake	B.	Late
___3.	Tell	C.	Kneed
___4.	Reaps	D.	Brained
___5.	Hand	E.	Tire

Number 63

___1.	Apple	A.	Score
___2.	Dire	B.	Eggs

____ 3. Dines   C. Odor
____ 4. Zoned   D. Eden
____ 5. Front   E. Remark

Number 64

____ 1. Ticks   A. Opted
____ 2. Fired   B. Drive
____ 3. Skin   C. Pin
____ 4. Train   D. Drop
____ 5. Cattle   E. Chicken

Number 65

____ 1. Sleet   A. Boat
____ 2. Fryer   B. Other
____ 3. Egg   C. Pest
____ 4. Neon   D. Remit
____ 5. Foot   E. Mill

Number 66

____ 1. Arch   A. Throat
____ 2. Door   B. Views
____ 3. House   C. Yemen
____ 4. First   D. Neigh
____ 5. Rose   E. Notre

Number 67

____ 1. Thorn   A. Dance
____ 2. Froth   B. Moor
____ 3. Sea   C. Wind
____ 4. Living   D. Right
____ 5. Bran   E. Loin

Number 68

_____ 1.   Sift   A.   Hurt
_____ 2.   Babe   B.   Eat
_____ 3.   Writs   C.   Post
_____ 4.   Sun   D.   Fight
_____ 5.   Iced   E.   Watch

Number 69

_____ 1.   Teddy   A.   House
_____ 2.   Cape   B.   Maker
_____ 3.   Sauce   C.   Graze
_____ 4.   Star   D.   Bare
_____ 5.   Wear   E.   Trouble

Number 70

_____ 1.   Peach   A.   Ideas
_____ 2.   Clam   B.   Down
_____ 3.   Military   C.   Skate
_____ 4.   Nile   D.   Haves
_____ 5.   Close   E.   Dealt

Number 71

_____ 1.   Weeps   A.   Lemon
_____ 2.   Shore   B.   Laugh
_____ 3.   Water   C.   Pole
_____ 4.   Some   D.   Night
_____ 5.   Shout   E.   Stakes

Number 72

_____ 1.   Reset   A.   Clear
_____ 2.   Forest   B.   Pipe

_____ 3. Votes
_____ 4. From
_____ 5. Kitchen

C. Letter
D. Skin
E. Fries

Number 73

_____ 1. Swap
_____ 2. Tooth
_____ 3. Gird
_____ 4. Rain
_____ 5. Blank

A. Prod
B. Nest
C. Shrub
D. Veers
E. Iron

Number 74

_____ 1. Human
_____ 2. Chicken
_____ 3. Disk
_____ 4. Shoe
_____ 5. Felt

A. Turn
B. Row
C. Begin
D. Terse
E. Scoop

Number 75

_____ 1. Purse
_____ 2. Class
_____ 3. Fire
_____ 4. Tills
_____ 5. Ports

A. Life
B. Gulp
C. Grin
D. Coat
E. Man

Number 76

_____ 1. None
_____ 2. User
_____ 3. Golf
_____ 4. Tail
_____ 5. Rout

A. Bus
B. Sign
C. Snip
D. Fire
E. Slink

Number 77

___1.	Scape	A.	Glass
___2.	Clasp	B.	Ship
___3.	Brief	C.	Lock
___4.	Step	D.	Out
___5.	Hoots	E.	Control

Number 78

___1.	Acre	A.	Hose
___2.	Army	B.	Scamp
___3.	Back	C.	Tribe
___4.	Sever	D.	Track
___5.	Horse	E.	Time

Number 79

___1.	Spot	A.	Throw
___2.	Stand	B.	Grease
___3.	Fort	C.	Pinto
___4.	Below	D.	Crow
___5.	Races	E.	Office

Number 80

___1.	Ruth	A.	Case
___2.	Trips	B.	Pride
___3.	Sitar	C.	Saber
___4.	Three	D.	Mining
___5.	Strut	E.	Worthy

Lost
Letters
Puzzles

These puzzles use a simple device to provide practice in recognizing a pattern that is not quite complete. In this case, one has to recognize the possibility of changing one word to another, by either dropping a letter or adding a letter. Since some words need an additional letter, some need to drop a letter, and some are correct as they are, the multiple paths to a solution require that a flexible approach be taken. There are ten of these puzzles.

Instructions: Match each word on the left with a word on the right. Matching is done on the basis of similar meaning. One word in each pair, however, is slightly incorrect. Either a letter is missing and must be added or there is one letter too many which must be deleted.

Since the three extra letters to be deleted are the same letters of the alphabet as the three letters to be added, you can think of each puzzle as containing three displaced or "lost" letters. By finding these letters and putting them where they belong, you can then easily match the words.

For each matching pair, one word is already correct and one is incorrect. The incorrect word in each pair may be on the left or on the right. Answers to the following puzzles begin on page 133.

Lost Letters Puzzles

Number 1

_____1. Bed   A   Slack

_____2. Avid   B.   Coat

_____3. Pants   C.   Help

_____4. Bag   D.   Ye

_____5. Yes   E.   Shoe

_____6. Push   F.   Vegetation

Number 2

_____1. Slap   A.   Change

_____2. Now   B.   Hack

_____3. Friend   C.   Negative

_____4. Bloom   D.   Beloved

_____5. Ear   E.   Dally

_____6. Falter   F.   Lower

Number 3

_____1. Gland   A.   Pleased

_____2. Decay   B.   Die

_____3. Girl   C.   Court

_____4. Wood   D.   Reside

_____5. Eat   E.   Mad

_____6. Well   F.   Riot

Number 4

_____1. Place   A.   Chubby

_____2. Close   B.   How

_____3. Wail   C.   Splash

_____4. Lump   D.   Stride

_____5.	Cut	E.	Hut
_____6.	Sold	F.	Aged

Number 5

_____1.	Chum	A.	Tint
_____2.	Give	B.	Build
_____3.	Boast	C.	Decrease
_____4.	Crate	D.	Rant
_____5.	Huge	E.	Bag
_____6.	Die	F.	Peal

Number 6

_____1.	Trap	A.	Bend
_____2.	Bold	B.	Trudge
_____3.	Trade	C.	Over
_____4.	Numerous	D.	Man
_____5.	Pasty	E.	Darling
_____6.	Mix	F.	Swamp

Number 7

_____1.	Crow	A.	Planet
_____2.	Burn	B.	Cube
_____3.	Die	C.	Plead
_____4.	Peel	D.	Brawl
_____5.	Hearth	E.	Car
_____6.	Metal	F.	Are

Number 8

_____1.	Fine	A.	Sell
_____2.	Wear	B.	Wrath
_____3.	Damp	C.	Twist

_____4.	Danger	D.	Curse
_____5.	Win	E.	West
_____6.	Limb	F.	Warm

Number 9

_____1.	Gather	A.	Quiet
_____2.	Yarn	B.	Spirit
_____3.	Tear	C.	Mass
_____4.	Host	D.	Long
_____5.	Stop	E.	Beast
_____6.	Tops	F.	Grip

Number 10

_____1.	Heart	A.	Weak
_____2.	Alarm	B.	Sufficient
_____3.	Fact	C.	Cave
_____4.	Sample	D.	Deed
_____5.	Desire	E.	Warm
_____6.	Rail	F.	Care

Regroup
Puzzles

These puzzles require associational flexibility. Creative thinking often requires that a person be able to see multiple possible associations between ideas and concepts. Tests of flexibility in word associations have been used to test for, and give training in, this type of flexible thinking. Regroup puzzles require that one associational "set" be abandoned in order to regroup the words in terms of other associations. These puzzles are longer than the others and require more time to complete each one. There are fifteen of these puzzles.

Instructions: Each puzzle consists of fifteen compound words, two-syllable words, or two-word phrases. The puzzle is solved by breaking each item into two parts and regrouping the parts so that there are an additional fifteen *different* compound words, two-syllable words, or two-word phrases. It is possible that you can regroup all of the items on a particular puzzle in some manner other than that given as the answer in the back of the book, but that is not likely to happen often.

To begin, pick a word (half of an associated pair) and try to find another word with which it is associated. For example, if two of the items were "scoutmaster" and "piecemeal," you could form "masterpiece" as a regrouped item and then look for words to associate with "scout" and "meal." Keep in mind that an apparently correct match may have to be changed if using it prevents you from being able to match all of the items. Answers to Regroup Puzzles begin on page 137.

Regroup Puzzles

Number 1

1. American Legion
2. Jackpot
3. Pig Latin
4. Stop sign
5. Scoutmaster
6. Foreign language
7. Ball game
8. Shotgun
9. Cockpit
10. Penknife
11. Eyepiece
12. Yellow jacket
13. Flower girl
14. Lifeboat
15. Stone wall

Number 2

1. Pole vault
2. Workbook
3. Egghead
4. Sidewalk
5. Bank president
6. Saddle soap
7. Green light
8. Catfish
9. Bread line
10. Vice squad

11.   Hornet nest   _____

12.   Boxcar   _____

13.   Hookworm   _____

14.   Switchboard   _____

15.   Corn patch   _____

Number 3

1.   Fire station   _____

2.   Independent judgment   _____

3.   Alarm clock   _____

4.   Backstage   _____

5.   Sunup   _____

6.   Field hand   _____

7.   Shutdown   _____

8.   Football coach   _____

9.   Secret Service   _____

10.   Daylight   _____

11.   Socket wrench   _____

12.   Grandfather clause   _____

13.   Monkeyshine   _____

14.   Milk shake   _____

15.   Bottle top   _____

Number 4

1.   Mail carrier   _____

2.   Little Rock   _____

3.   Punch bowl   _____

4.   General Electric   _____

5.   Bagman   _____

6.   Dishpan   _____

7. Train track _____

8. Hudson Bay _____

9. Peter Rabbit _____

10. Stool pigeon _____

11. Sugar pine _____

12. Major league _____

13. Window washer _____

14. Needlework _____

15. Foot race _____

Number 5

1. Redskin _____

2. Firsthand _____

3. Money order _____

4. Catfish _____

5. Top hat _____

6. Card file _____

7. Wild West _____

8. Shortstop _____

9. Bandaid _____

10. Sign post _____

11. Pickpocket _____

12. Standpoint _____

13. Sea shell _____

14. Singletree _____

15. Ice cream _____

Number 6

1. Safety pin _____

2. Brush fire _____

3. Place kick   _____
4. Touchdown   _____
5. Hold back   _____
6. Shoulder strap   _____
7. Town meeting   _____
8. Toothless   _____
9. Hogtie   _____
10. Frostbite   _____
11. Playhouse   _____
12. Cracker Jack   _____
13. Softball   _____
14. Background   _____
15. Razorblade   _____

Number 7

1. Angleworm   _____
2. School year   _____
3. Bullfight   _____
4. Drumbeat   _____
5. Jet plane   _____
6. Jump rope   _____
7. Woodcut   _____
8. Leapfrog   _____
9. Bath oil   _____
10. Geometry teacher   _____
11. Lay eggs   _____
12. Songbird   _____
13. Outright   _____

14.	Set bail	_____
15.	Up tight	_____

Number 8

1.	Ocean breeze	_____
2.	Talk show	_____
3.	Carport	_____
4.	Ice water	_____
5.	Power line	_____
6.	Monkey business	_____
7.	Windbreaker	_____
8.	Manhole	_____
9.	Trademark	_____
10.	Downstream	_____
11.	Flat-footed	_____
12.	Indian moccasin	_____
13.	Right way	_____
14.	Baby book	_____
15.	Spider web	_____

Number 9

1.	Private detective	_____
2.	Millstream	_____
3.	Guardrail	_____
4.	Jailbird	_____
5.	Softball	_____
6.	Hammer lock	_____
7.	Dry cell	_____
8.	Road trip	_____

   9.   Draw blood   _____

  10.   Warehouse   _____

  11.   Jawbone   _____

  12.   Overbearing   _____

  13.   Hound dog   _____

  14.   Sawbuck   _____

  15.   Gulf Coast   _____

Number 10

   1.   Price freeze   _____

   2.   Redcap   _____

   3.   Reverend Graham   _____

   4.   Perry Mason   _____

   5.   Oversight   _____

   6.   Curbstone   _____

   7.   Right Guard   _____

   8.   Money market   _____

   9.   Pistol range   _____

  10.   Hot water   _____

  11.   Love letter   _____

  12.   Rear admiral   _____

  13.   Hush puppy   _____

  14.   Soda cracker   _____

  15.   Eye opener   _____

Number 11

   1.   Ladyfinger   _____

   2.   Topcoat   _____

   3.   Hose pipe   _____

4. Dreamland   _____
5. Hair net   _____
6. Paper plate   _____
7. Pantywaist   _____
8. Footboard   _____
9. Index card   _____
10. Sideline   _____
11. Home front   _____
12. Heavyweight   _____
13. Yard party   _____
14. Newsprint   _____
15. Cut up   _____

Number 12

1. Spring fever   _____
2. Game laws   _____
3. Galley proof   _____
4. Forefather   _____
5. Windmill   _____
6. Mark time   _____
7. Slavemaster   _____
8. Moreover   _____
9. Instep   _____
10. Yellowtail   _____
11. Birthstone   _____
12. Never mind   _____
13. Bombshell   _____
14. Well-read   _____
15. Groundwork   _____

Number 13

1. Buckskin   _____
2. Township   _____
3. Sweetgum   _____
4. Vice president   _____
5. Road scraper   _____
6. Creekfish   _____
7. Potato chip   _____
8. Sky diver   _____
9. Bubble bath   _____
10. Shotput   _____
11. Roy Rogers   _____
12. Housewife   _____
13. Runner-up   _____
14. Cleveland Indians   _____
15. Roommate   _____

Number 14

1. Purse snatcher   _____
2. Policeman   _____
3. Apple butter   _____
4. Everybody   _____
5. Bell pepper   _____
6. Hopper car   _____
7. Dogwood   _____
8. Mint mark   _____
9. Cowboy   _____
10. Pull strings   _____
11. Trade fair   _____

12. Crab grass   _____
13. Pet duck   _____
14. Plaything   _____
15. Fly catcher   _____

Number 15

1.   Silent partner   _____
2.   Stickpin   _____
3.   Main Street   _____
4.   Blind alley   _____
5.   Outside   _____
6.   Night light   _____
7.   Corn meal   _____
8.   Off-color   _____
9.   Crossbow   _____
10. Limewater   _____
11. Square dance   _____
12. Cattail   _____
13. Shipyard   _____
14. Pop-eyed   _____
15. Rolling stone   _____

Creativity in Everyday Life

As you tried to solve the puzzles in this book, you probably found that you did best when you approached them in a playful mood. In such a mood, you probably found it easier to see an unusual connection or non-obvious relationship. Your playful mental set contributed to flexibility and thereby to success in solving the puzzles.

In considering how you can live a more creative everyday life, you should ask yourself how often you approach your daily problems or personal goals in a playful and flexible frame of mind. Too often, perhaps, you may approach your work with a mental set so serious that the end result is rigid thinking and unimaginative attempts to solve your problems.

As a personal experiment, pick five or six problems or tasks with which you have been having difficulty, and try to think about them in the same playful frame of mind with which you approached the puzzles in this book. First write down the problems, as you see them, so that you will know exactly what it is you are trying to solve. Then, in a playful and unhurried manner, try to generate as many possible solutions as you can think of. Consider all ideas that occur to you even if they are impractical, wild, half-baked or far-fetched. Treat your problems as puzzles and assume that there are probably creative solutions you haven't yet "seen." In other words, approach the problems with the expectancy that there are aha!-type solutions just waiting to be found.

If a particular problem has you blocked, leave it and go to one of the others. Skip around from one problem to another as you skipped around from one puzzle item to another. As soon as you lose your playful mood or feel blocked, leave your list of problems and come back to them later. Consider them as unsolved puzzles to think about or play with from time to time. As soon as you come up with a solution or even a slightly better answer to the problem, mark it off and add a new problem to your list. Even minor insights or solutions are important, especially at first, since they will encourage you to continue with the technique until it becomes natural for you to approach your problems in a confident and flexible frame of mind.

By trying this technique with various types of problems, you can greatly increase your own power of creative or aha! thinking. As you learn to think more creatively you will find yourself willing to take on more ambitious problems and challenges because you will have more faith in your ability to find creative solutions.

Answers to Embedded Words Puzzles

No. 1

1D Question everyone—Ask all
2C Capable devil—Able demon
3B Quarrel—Run-in
4E Something all members of my family have in common—Our name
5A Not enough out—Too in

No. 2

1B Take Theodore out of the game—Rest Ted
2D Every pain—Each ache
3E Story for Pre-Easter—Lent tale
4A Notice grass—Spot pot
5C Children's request to be hugged—Hold us

No. 3

1E   Unhappy insect—Sad ant
2B   Appropriate bright color—Apt red
3D   Tiny tail—Wee end
4A   Something acne may do—Pit chin
5C   Attending disturbance—At riot

No. 4

1B   Consume almost a dozen—Eat ten
2C   Royal Family—King kin
3E   Fool Kenneth—Trick Ken
4A   Billboard—Road ad
5D   Price of vase—Urn tab

Answers to Flexibility Puzzles

No. 1

1C Bud get—Pick a rose early
2D Man if old—May be grandfather
3E Noah's creation—New ark
4B Filling (and) the bill—Two things obtained from dentist
5A Far-sighted surgeon—Long distance operator

No. 2

1D Ground hog—Sausage
2A Peer group—Spectators
3B Historian—Past master

4E   Loco motive—Calls for plea of insanity

5C   For give and for get—Draw names at
Christmas time

No. 3

1C   Bulldozer training—Grade school

2D   Is hare—Bugs Bunny

3A   Back burners—Rear range

4E   Marks man's hip—Gives tattoo where it won't
show

5B   Wee ding—Comes from small bell

No. 4

1B   Seat rip—Embarrassing tear

2E   Defective cards—Unsuited

3A   Pro portion—Half a debate

4D   Fill silo with wheat—Pour in grain

5C   Fall short—Early winter

No. 5

1D   Attach—Pin to

2C   Cereal bowl—Bran dish

3E   N.Y.M.P.H. (New York miles per hour)—Very
few in Manhattan traffic

4B   Box (eye) lid—Give black eye

5A   Freeze—Form ice

No. 6

1E   Make up the difference—Pale and colorful
faces

2C   George Washington—On the buck head (picture
on dollar bill)

3B   Out rigger—Crooked umpire
4A   Al Smith said he would be elected president
       —Al lied
5D   R.I. defender—Providence attorney

No. 7

1D   Second hand—Very brief applause
2C   String bass—Keep your catch
3E   Myself—The me
4A   "I've never told a girl this before"—
       International date line
5B   Snowy slope—Ski Place

No. 8

1C   Double deck—Knock down twin
2B   Being too truthful—Under lying
3D   Develop self-discipline—Whip poor will
4A   Care taker—Recipient of foreign aid
5E   Par able—Needs no handicap

No. 9

1A   S.C. owl—Southeastern bird
2C   Bump into dog—Ram pup
3E   A tease—One who kids around
4B   Break fast products—Poorly make goods
5D   Cover charge—Insulate a wire

No. 10

1E   Speak well—Remark ably
2C   List-less—Buying on impulse
3B   Results in fall—Ski tangle

4A   Not ours—Doesn't belong to us
5D   General assembly—Pentagon staff meeting

No. 11

1B   Hands—Go in gloves
2A   Gun runner—Act of careless starter
3E   Pass time—When you can't score running
4C   To count up—To tally
5D   Wildcat driller—Hunts oil

No. 12

1C   Take the lead—Steal metal
2D   Rabbit ears—Are long and listen for dogs
3E   Pa rents—We don't own a home
4B   Miss the ball—Catch air
5A   Let us begin—We start

No. 13

1D   To O.K.—To approve
2E   McKinley's Peak—Highest in North America
3A   Mini-mum—Short silence
4B   Small Russian on front of car—Little Red
      Riding Hood
5C   Foundation—House holds

No. 14

1D   Baby carriage—Part for small typewriter
2C   S.E. town—Jacksonville
3E   Shift allegiance—Wear only dresses that hang
      straight

4A   Put bend in trail—Warp lane
5B   Pointed tail—Imp end

No. 15

1E   Re-move—Cheat at checkers
2D   Notes to pen—Letters to write
3C   Gouge leg—Shin dig
4B   Neck and neck race—affectionate people
5A   Support indifferently—Half back

No. 16

1B   Roosters' gaze—At hens
2E   Gardener's fear—Maybe I get weeds
3D   Moment for making amends—Atone time
4A   Back order—Command to retreat
5C   Olds lacks—Cadillac's price and prestige

No. 17

1D   Search Harold for weapon—Hal Frisk
2A   Air Force dance—Base ball
3E   Change tires—Progress is fatiguing
4B   As light—No heavier
5C   Ten seal arms—Almost a dozen flippers

No. 18

1B   Ton arrow—Would require a very large bow
2C   Two—One and the same
3D   Worry—Makes the head lines
4A   Stay happy, pup—Wag on
5E   Mad rid—Cure insanity

No. 19

1D   Abdomen—Naval base
2C   Coo king—Chief dove
3A   Traditional—Custom built
4E   Lie down—Change planes
5B   No bridge—Can't get across river

No. 20

1B   Mild red—Pink
2D   Break through—Time to go back to work
3E   Quick change artist—Pickpocket
4A   Stops pout—Pulls in lips
5C   Leaning slightly—On brief diet

No. 21

1C   Rent the penthouse—Top lease
2E   Priest who hears confessions—Director of
     admissions
3D   Run a Long—To win office in Louisiana
4A   Am I able?—Self-doubt
5B   For tresses—Curlers

No. 22

1C   Roll ins—Lucky basketball shots
2D   Wooden steps—Fir stairs
3E   Test-tube babies—A lab a Ma
4A   Star town—Hollywood
5B   Approach—Go at

No. 23

1B   Enlarges hen pen—Doubles coop
2C   Pass port—Share wine

3A   Rig ht.—Wear elevated shoes
4E   Falling star—Champion skydiver
5D   Cotton gin—Doesn't taste like rye

No. 24

1D   Fold corners—For bashful sheep
2E   Unable to mimic—Can't ape
3C   Once anxious—In the past tense
4A   Emergency brakes—Coast guard
5B   Bet here—Race track window

No. 25

1E   Vice lord—Sin king
2A   Coin operated—Very cheap surgery
3D   Snake highway—Boa rd.
4B   Population problem—Over-bearing parents
5C   Go N.E.—To get from Houston to New York

No. 26

1D   Hi Jack—What not to say to the ripper
2E   Land office—Be elected
3B   For tune—Song of support
4A   Eating an apple—Makes core
5C   The Federal Reserve—Buck board

No. 27

1C   Exile monarch—Ban king
2E   P.E. ace—Star performer in physical
      education
3B   Speed reader—Highway patrolman
4A   Bar racks—Soap dishes
5D   Fla. grant—Land given by Spanish king

No. 28

1E   Out growth—Double play

2A   Join the Waves—For a Navy career, girls

3D   Ali as—Like the heavyweight boxer

4B   Slow ticket salesman—Line backer

5C   Cut classes—Bayonet practice

No. 29

1D   Noel coward—Child afraid of Santa

2B   Lumber company—Drunks taking a walk

3A   Mis-apprehension—False arrest

4C   Poe, try—Attempt it, Edgar

5E   Alaskan urban area—Metro Nome

No. 30

1D   Boxing round—Starts with a bell

2C   Proof read—Look at photograph

3E   Committed to the local electorate—Home ward bound

4A   Fine for public nudity—No-cover charge

5B   Hit chain—cuff links

No. 31

1D   Detectives' dance—Private eye ball

2C   Holding company—Refusing to say good-bye

3B   End anger—Cease being mad

4E   Earn loathing—Win disgust

5A   Rust—Car rot

No. 32

1C   Better half—Score above average

2E   Drill sergeant—Private tutor

3D   Blood's hot—Is passionate
4B   For mild punishment—Light switch
5A   Leg end—Ankle

No. 33

1D   Get up tight—Fail to sleep it off
2C   Evaluate Russian plane—Mig rate
3A   Ice milk—Not ice cream
4B   Short time for book—Minutes to read
5E   Blackboard—Re-mark-able

No. 34

1E   Take turns—Steal part of a race track
2A   Not sob right—Cry improperly
3D   A week is seven—Days
4C   Tear up urban areas—Scar cities
5B   Start a gain—Begin overeating

No. 35

1D   A red wet rust—May be found on old
     submarines
2A   Job change for magazine writer—*True* to
     Life
3E   Sunlit—Ray on
4C   Sit on—Put an end to
5B   Oppose the BBC—Cross English Channel

No. 36

1C   Go motoring—Drives take
2E   Date palm—Where to put the flowers or candy
3B   Ram parts—Bump heads

4A   Eyes ore—Looks at mine
5D   Notable—Worthy of notice

No. 37

1B   Double header—Crooked coin
2C   Nagging wife—Man ager
3E   Skip practice—Requires a rope
4A   Auto accident information—Skid angle
5D   Wide spread—King Ranch

No. 38

1C   Car trails—Roads
2D   Increase in amount of military service—Hitch hike
3A   Stay, Mom—Ma, linger
4E   From Betsy stems—Design of our flag
5B   June 21—Fly-by night

No. 39

1D   Get ready to drive—Set tee
2E   Re-pair—Marry again
3C   Oriental customs agents—Chinese checkers
4A   Tot ally—Teddy bear
5B   Drum major—Narrow academic specialty

No. 40

1E   Quick look around—Brief case
2C   Ad just—Fair commercial
3B   Must stay in base path—Slide rule
4A   Coin-cide—Killing money
5D   Sham rock—Imitation diamond

No. 41

1C Fellow gangster—Brother hood
2D Spouse—Human I mated
3A Buys large sizes and a basketball—Shopping center
4E Type writer—Novelist
5B Elegant breathing—Fancy pants

No. 42

1B Correspondence—Trading post
2D Hurt Roosevelt—Pain Ted
3E Mustache—Tickles the one kissed
4A Shells hock—Pawn ammunition
5C Small joke—Ha bit

No. 43

1D Beg increase—Plea for more
2B Off ice hours—Hockey player's leisure time
3A Horse—A mount
4E Excessive use of articles—A-the-ism
5C Struck out—Batter whipped

No. 44

1B Pocket change—Alteration of pool table
2A Re-sound—Echo
3D Life raft—Overpopulated
4E A ship—Enters ports
5C Hear thunder—Listen to storm

No. 45

1D Big buddy—Fat ally
2E A bad tool—Bum pliars

3B   Tops ail—Good medicine
4C   Strike cup—Hit chalice
5A   Cur rent—Kennel fee

No. 46

1E   Imp act—Naughty deed
2D   Cement mixer—Repair kitchen utensil
3B   Expensive wife—Fur lover
4A   Ask questions at a duel—Trouble shooter
5C   Tan gent—Male lifeguard

No. 47

1C   Sub division—Purpose of depth charge
2E   Peanut butter—Undersized goat
3B   Boy shave—Defuzzing
4A   Relatives look on—Kin gape
5D   I deal aces—I'll give you good cards

No. 48

1E   Combination lock—Part wig and part natural
2D   Wet each one—To put out matches
3A   Thermal underwear—Shorts hot
4C   Call your shot—Pick pocket
5B   Small cloth or paper—Kid napkin

No. 49

1B   Continue—Go on
2C   Melting pot—Exercising
3A   They are dwarfs or fairies—Them's elves
4E   Betray—Deceive
5D   Spanking—Seat belts

No. 50

1C   Advanced standing—Walked
2D   Printing press—Crowded first grade
3E   Genial president—Warm Ike
4B   Last thing pulled in puppet show—Bow string
5A   Wee plate—For tiny servings

No. 51

1D   Waste basket—Make shot after buzzer
2C   Trigger revolt—Buck Rogers
3A   Score touchdown and extra point—Get seven
4E   Car tag new—Shiny license plate
5B   Go to get her—Fetch the girl

No. 52

1D   Thin king—Skinny monarch
2A   No tread—Beware of blowout
3E   Superior court—Woo the boss
4C   Save electricity—Less ons
5B   Lawyer's office—Bar room

No. 53

1E   Moll—Girl hood
2D   Foot board—Ski
3A   I'll marry about Christmas—Dec. I mate
4B   Ball ads—Sell sporting goods
5C   One girl getting all the dates—A men corner

No. 54

1C   Under-ground—Cheap coffee
2D   Send message to officials—Wire wheels

3B   An active people—A do nation
4A   Dresses went in old days—To Ma toes
5E   Noise of a boy—A lad din

No. 55

1B   Rock music—Lullaby
2D   Take charge—Taxi fare
3E   Be a con man—Learn to swindle
4A   Cats kill—Birds
5C   Having sympathy—Co-aching

No. 56

1E   Doctors house—Changes residence
2D   Land mark—Tire track on runway
3C   Manila folder—Oriental lawn chair
4B   Sun dries—Clothes on line
5A   Sharp tongued—Dart mouth

No. 57

1B   Stitch—Hem lock
2C   Office of the boss—Fire place
3E   Growing a part—Balding
4A   Mends broken heart?—Ticker tape
5D   Very bad golf shot—Missing links

No. 58

1D   A girl yearns—For mink
2C   The fatted calf—Sign of the bicycle rider
3E   Asp halt—Snake stop

4A   Compassionate comrade—Kind red
5B   Best rain—Follows a drought

No. 59

1B   Draw poker—Dead gunfighter
2C   Don't betray country—No treason
3E   Preside as judge—Work bench
4A   The last is Sue—Slow Susan
5D   Recapping shop—Tread mill

No. 60

1D   Alter natives—Missionary's job
2B   New Orleans rock—La. stone
3A   Aim of filibuster—Perpetual motion
4E   V for Victory—Roman basketball team
5C   Tend to my watch and I'll tend to yours—
      Trade winds

No. 61

1A   L.A. goon—West Coast thug
2E   Mush room—Space for sled dogs to run
3D   Truck like—Vanish
4B   Be off key—Mis-sing
5C   Examination for amnesia—Blank check

No. 62

1E   Tom—Cat's paw
2C   Sweet roll—Loaded dice
3B   Cabbage sprout—Head start
4A   Power lines—Chain of command
5D   Not at own house—Visiting

No. 63

1C   Type setter—Irish
2E   Boo King—Did I scare you, Sire?
3A   A drill sergeant doesn't say—In formation please
4D   Crowded fishing—Stream lined
5B   Make shift—Trade cars

No. 64

1B   Out of bounds—Untied
2D   Have a double—Be twin
3A   Wish to board—Want on
4C   Ignorant of women soldiers—No WAC knowledge
5E   Sport scar—Show off old injury

No. 65

1D   Dec. ade—Christmas drink
2E   Have no bearing—Faulty skates
3A   Star tout—Job for press agent
4B   Nonprofit organizations—Bar gains
5C   Sound proof—Conclusive evidence

No. 66

1C   Size up—Gain weight
2E   Plea sure—Ask confidently
3A   Ill suited—Wearing hospital gown
4B   Wishing well—Pleases fairy godmother
5D   I'm so tardy—I so late

No. 67

1D   Under stand—Slouch
2E   Short coming—Rotting insulation

3B   Holds cue cards—Line coach
4A   Cured—Well made
5C   Tails pin—Kids at birthday party

No. 68

1B   Pull with wrecker—Tow it
2C   Slap Happy—Mistreat a dwarf
3D   Grand slam—Angry exit
4E   A.C. cost—Electricity bill
5A   Striped bass—In prison choir

No. 69

1E   Fall through—December 21
2D   Go toil—Start work
3B   Short wave—Brief greeting
4A   League of Nations—U.N. like
5C   Prop a gate—Make a temporary barnyard
     repair

No. 70

1C   Who not to loan soap to—Bar keeper
2B   Medieval hero—Star knight
3E   Sound better—Plays the odds
4D   Pick pocket—Needed by guitar player
5A   Frail knees and elbows—Light sockets

No. 71

1B   Divorce—Wed rift
2C   Snaps hot—Trouble with shorts just out of
     the dryer
3A   Roofer—completes top

4E   Tend to fumble—Green backs
5D   Poor furlough—Leave a mess

No. 72

1C   Dear Santa Claus—Re presents
2E   Got hiccups—Drink water for cure
3B   Circle up—Be a ring
4A   A Brooklyn rabbit—N.Y. long ears
5D   First ray—Dawn

No. 73

1E   Fire department—Get rid of the whole group
2D   None's old—All are young
3A   Snack bar—Strict diet
4B   Walk back and forth—To pace
5C   Toy pistol—Cap size

No. 74

1D   Hair mussed up—de-parted
2A   Bonnet for mother hog—Sow hat
3E   A.F. raid—Bombing mission
4C   S.W. Eden—Part of Adam's garden
5B   Looks at locomotive—Eyes train

No. 75

1C   Taste swine—Eat pork
2E   I'm feeling good—Am O.K.
3D   Gets a wag—Pup pet
4A   Maxi-mum—Top secret
5B   S.C. rolls—Southern bread

No. 76

1E   Be at—Attend
2C   May have little snakes—Pair of moccasins
3D   Pull over—Loss of influence
4A   No trace—Vanished
5B   Breaking lass—Causing girl to go broke

No. 77

1B   "F" able—Capable of flunking
2D   Cross examination—Job for eye doctor
3E   Air craft—Announcing
4A   Paint that shows—Top coat
5C   Floats—Lighter fluid

No. 78

1C   Book Mark—Schedule Biblical writer
2D   Widen the street—Chip off the old block
3A   Just ice—South Pole
4E   Mat tresses—Get hair wet
5B   Kite—Fly paper

No. 79

1B   Falling rain—Drizzle
2E   Fifth amendment—Water down bottle of whiskey
3D   Included in vehicle tally—Pontiac count
4A   Agricultural—Of farms
5C   Hum—Sing almost

No. 80

1C   Cat chat—Persian conversing with Siamese
2D   Jet set—Quick hatch

3B   Seven come eleven—Roll call
4E   Not absent—Present
5A   Name dropping in Monaco—Saying Grace

No. 81

1D   Out and out—Double play
2C   Monologue—Solid state
3B   Parallel bars—Bourbon Street
4E   Ha shed—Fun house
5A   Lenient sentence—Off light

No. 82

1E   Snow bank—Get loan without collateral
2D   Rear view—Book by Dr. Spock
3C   For alto get her—She has a good voice
4B   Fallout fits—In an atomic nightmare
5A   Put out the best silver—Trust company

No. 83

1B   Fighter plane—Hopefully not horizontal
2C   Banker—Fancy pool shooter
3A   Ref uses—Whistle
4D   Electrical inspector—Circuit judge
5E   Bullet—Article in magazine

No. 84

1E   Bet rigger happy—When fight thrown
2C   Old tub—Ring bearer
3A   Paratrooper who forgets chute—First down
4B   A tangle—Snarl
5D   Dressing room—Inside the turkey

No. 85

1B   After work—Post office
2D   Break ground—Corral
3E   Import ant—Foreign bug
4C   Mixed reviews—Fair play
5A   Left one when facing northwest—S.W. ear

No. 86

1E   Cell mate—Pen pal
2D   Mar row—Plow sloppily
3A   Eye lashes—Stern looks
4B   Where fanatics congregate—In sects
5C   Fund a mental hospital—Give money for a
good cause

No. 87

1D   No strikes—Bowl awfully
2C   Old Ironsides—Hard ship
3B   Jump suit—Settle out of court
4E   Put on the dog—Tease the pup
5A   Has will power—Rich uncle

No. 88

1C   My taxi—Cab I net
2E   Mild cheese—Results in faint smile
3B   For help at Capitol—See page
4A   Quick delivery of fishing gear—Flying tackle
5D   Foreign aid—U.S. grant

No. 89

1E   Too much play—Tires kid
2C   All single births—No twin

3D   Bug a crooner—Rub Bing the wrong way

4B   Take the by-pass—Dodge city

5A   Virginia to Florida—The S.E.

No. 90

1D   Ex ample—No longer enough

2E   Man I cure—My patient

3A   Refuse to be married—Strike a match

4B   How to express pain—Yell Ow

5C   Spinning rod—Baton

No. 91

1C   Bar on age—Exclude minors

2D   Just losses—Never a gain

3E   Tow his key—Purpose of Franklin's kite

4A   Wind velocity—Air's pace

5B   Lockjaw—Lip stick

No. 92

1B   Never the less—Which piece of pie taken by
     boy

2C   Leave third—Steal away home

3E   Our group naughty—We evil

4A   Unders—Pl. under

5D   Restrain—Hold back

No. 93

1B   Use hair spray—Set a part

2C   St. Amp—Patron saint of electricians?

3D   Second rate—Very quick evaluation

4E   Ace through ten—Pre-face

5A   All owed—Bankrupt

No. 94

1D Checking account—Cross examination
2C A fore said—Warns other golfers
3E Bring up, rear—Raise raise
4A Easy dieting—Fast asleep
5B Stirring and drinking—Still life

No. 95

1E Rug by stands—Artificial turf
2D Batting average—Normal winking
3A A.C. cord—Power line
4B State fair—Say it pretty well
5C Holiday—Day break

No. 96

1D Boxer's strategy—Floor plan
2E Show disapproval at opera—Rock bass
3B Come to order—Wake up!
4C High and low—Depressed drunk
5A Shoot straight—Healthy plant

No. 97

1B Skywriting—Suspended sentence
2D Far-fetched—Imported
3E Extreme egotism—I flawless
4A Cavalry—Rein force
5C If you don't make any outs—Bat on

No. 98

1C Washer woman—Lady plumber
2E Above board—Rafter
3D Re-fuse—Make electrical repair

4A   Person stared down—First batter
5B   Finished with baby talk—Goo done

No. 99

1E   High noon—Start drinking early or quit late
2D   At loose ends—Where to pass
3A   Official residence—Legal pad
4C   Harvest a fruit—Reap pears
5B   Written after Fargo or Bismarck—Comma N.D.

No. 100

1D   Early evening—Quick revenge
2E   Opposed to painting—Against art
3B   Always on our side—Automatic ally
4A   Pauses—Stops
5C   Sear chrome—Burn car trim

Answers to Anagram Matching Puzzles

No. 1

1C. Sirloin steak
2A. Santa Claus
3D. Lamb chops
4E. Outer space
5B. Square dance

No. 2

1E. Rangoon, Burma
2C. Clark Gable
3A. Grab bag
4B. Eager beaver
5D. Roommate

No. 3

1D. Shave cream
2C. Atlantic Ocean
3E. Balsa wood
4B. Chain saw
5A. Saint Peter

No. 4

1D. Pancake
2E. Railroad
3C. Beanstalk
4B. Akron, Ohio
5A. Peach fuzz

No. 5

1D.	Top secret
2C.	Cornbread
3A.	Trail boss
4E.	Brick mason
5B.	Fingernails

No. 6

1C.	Beauty salon
2D.	Brute force
3E.	Hair spray
4B.	Soap bubble
5A.	Great Dane

No. 7

1A.	Batman
2C.	Cedar Rapids
3B.	Steak sauce
4E.	Turncoats
5D.	Nickname

No. 8

1D.	Paleface
2C.	Blind dates
3A.	Bus fare
4B.	Phase out
5E.	Ice skate

No. 9

1E.	Real life
2D.	Stew meat
3C.	First rate
4A.	Task force
5B.	Navy blue

No. 10

1C.	Ski lodge
2D.	Flood tide
3E.	Solid state
4A.	Knee jerk
5B.	Air rifle

No. 11

1B.	Sand piles
2A.	Grape wines
3E.	Lose weight
4C.	Bird nest
5D.	Golf cart

No. 12

1A.	Full grown
2E.	Pool table
3B.	Bluebeard
4D.	About-face
5C.	False alarm

No. 13

1D.	Naked eye
2B.	Drag race

No. 14

1B.	Nightmare
2D.	Tapeworm

3C.	Stagecoach		3A.	Run along
4E.	Speakeasy		4C.	Spring thaw
5A.	Hot plate		5E.	Last chance

No. 15			No. 16	
1C.	Bootstrap		1A.	Blue Ridge
2D.	Seat belts		2E.	Denim jacket
3A.	Apple cider		3C.	Slipped disk
4E.	Screwdriver		4B.	Thereafter
5B.	Blood clot		5D.	Flesh wound

No. 17			No. 18	
1E.	Milepost		1A.	Stop sign
2A.	Police siren		2E.	Skinflint
3C.	North Pole		3C.	Plum tree
4B.	Class notes		4B.	Trout stream
5D.	West Point		5D.	Tire tread

No. 19			No. 20	
1B.	Hair braid		1C.	Dealt cards
2C.	Bareback		2E.	Dual control
3A.	Clean slate		3D.	Airplane
4D.	Crash helmet		4A.	Toothpaste
5E.	Front page		5B.	Gearshift

No. 21			No. 22	
1E.	Snare drum		1B.	Snap shut
2B.	Hot seat		2C.	Sugar beets
3A.	Billy goat		3E.	Bowl game
4D.	Ink stain		4A.	Full speed
5C.	Small fry		5D.	Corkscrew

No. 23

1C. Daredevil
2A. Spendthrift
3D. Freeloader
4E. Nevermore
5B. Hitchhikes

No. 25

1D. Fishhooks
2B. Split-level
3A. Senior prom
4C. Glass beads
5E. Saber-toothed

No. 27

1B. Shade tree
2E. Dear Sir
3D. Great Lakes
4A. Sneak preview
5C. Mental lapse

No. 29

1C. Sharpshooter
2A. Palm tree
3E. Part-time
4B. Indian tribe
5D. Death blow

No. 31

1B. Salt mines
2A. Last straw

No. 24

1A. Evil eye
2C. Snow tire
3E. Morse code
4B. Paper route
5D. Frostbite

No. 26

1B. Shoelaces
2D. Lackluster
3C. Outcast
4E. Drawback
5A. Stargazer

No. 28

1E. Veal cutlet
2A. Spearmint
3B. Life raft
4C. Somewhat
5D. Solar eclipse

No. 30

1B. Cowboy boots
2C. Scorecard
3E. Livestock
4D. Field trip
5A. Slide rule

No. 32

1C. Buffalo herds
2E. Notebook

3D.	Tap dance	3A.	Dense smoke
4C.	Cloudburst	4B.	Doomsday
5E.	Ice picks	5D.	Sleepwalker

No. 33

No. 34

1D.	Fishing reel	1B.	Seven dwarfs
2B.	Seaports	2C.	Heartfelt
3C.	Live wire	3D.	Time bomb
4A.	Lemon tree	4E.	Sunrise
5E.	Golden Rule	5A.	Notre Dame

No. 35

No. 36

1D.	Brake fluid	1C.	Slack off
2E.	Anthill	2A.	Death Valley
3B.	Wage scale	3E.	Bicycle pedal
4C.	Charm bracelet	4D.	Car radio
5A.	Coast Guard	5B.	Right angle

No. 37

No. 38

1B.	Chinatown	1C.	Sad sack
2D.	Grade school	2B.	Fatback
3E.	Eggheads	3A.	Squad car
4A.	Magic wand	4E.	Steam heat
5C.	Archangel	5D.	Maple syrup

No. 39

No. 40

1E.	Wiseacre	1E.	Ocean perch
2C.	Smack-dab	2A.	Tie clasp
3D.	Fair share	3C.	Muckrake
4B.	Wake up	4D.	Lean-to
5A.	Layer cake	5B.	Meanwhile

No. 41

1A.	Windowpane
2D.	Teardrop
3B.	Organ grinder
4C.	Lamp shade
5E.	Roman Empire

No. 43

1C.	Oil wells
2B.	Open door
3E.	Sent forth
4A.	Ski lift
5D.	Wrong number

No. 45

1D.	Throwback
2E.	Slipshod
3A.	Stool pigeon
4C.	Lifeboats
5B.	Smokestack

No. 47

1C.	Mass media
2D.	Amen Corner
3A.	Wardrobe
4E.	Shipshape
5B.	Take place

No. 49

1C.	Early bird
2E.	Steam ship

No. 42

1D.	Paintbrush
2C.	Sweat gland
3E.	Smash hit
4A.	Salt lick
5B.	Bear traps

No. 44

1B.	Lone Ranger
2D.	Evermore
3A.	Rosebush
4C.	Right wing
5E.	Iron lungs

No. 46

1A.	Pinto beans
2E.	Teaspoon
3C.	Strait-laced
4B.	Cape Cod
5D.	Cigar box

No. 48

1B.	Horseflies
2A.	Trademark
3D.	Dairy farm
4E.	Earthquake
5C.	Oatmeal

No. 50

1C.	Slave ship
2A.	Weather vane

3B. Save face
4D. Bathrobe
5A. Ink blot

3D. Taste bud
4E. Stray cat
5B. Heart throb

No. 51

1E. Ice cold
2D. Shock troops
3C. Marine Corps
4A. Short-lived
5B. Swordfish

No. 52

1D. Peptic ulcer
2E. Sonic boom
3A. Scot-free
4C. Line drive
5B. Sawdust

No. 53

1B. Past tense
2D. French fries
3C. Slowpokes
4E. Home owner
5A. Purse strings

No. 54

1A. Keep house
2C. Shore line
3B. Spine tingling
4E. Flagstone
5D. Jump rope

No. 55

1D. Fire tower
2E. First base
3A. Beverly Hills
4C. Spillway
5B. Water polo

No. 56

1B. Straw votes
2C. Night light
3E. Soothsayer
4A. Shopping list
5D. Turntable

No. 57

1E. Breakdown
2A. Cadet Corps
3B. Forward march
4D. Put aside
5C. Hearsay

No. 58

1B. Drumbeat
2D. Carefree
3A. Clambake
4E. Fair Deal
5C. Leakproof

No. 59		*No. 60*	
1C.	Lame duck	1D.	Panel truck
2A.	Late show	2C.	Namesake
3D.	Shipmate	3B.	Pear tree
4E.	Far East	4A.	Wastebasket
5B.	Sharkskin	5E.	Water glass

No. 61		*No. 62*	
1B.	Sweetheart	1D.	Hare-brained
2C.	Pin-up	2C.	Weak-kneed
3E.	Relay switch	3B.	Telltale
4D.	Nearby	4E.	Spare tire
5A.	Texas ranger	5A.	Handcuffs

No. 63		*No. 64*	
1A.	Apple cores	1C.	Stickpin
2D.	Dire need	2E.	Fried chicken
3E.	Snide remark	3B.	Skin diver
4B.	Dozen eggs	4A.	Train depot
5C.	Front door	5D.	Cattle prod

No. 65		*No. 66*	
1E.	Steel mill	1C.	Archenemy
2A.	Ferry boat	2D.	Door hinge
3D.	Egg timer	3B.	Housewives
4B.	None other	4E.	First tenor
5C.	Footstep	5A.	Sore throat

No. 67		*No. 68*	
1C.	North wind	1D.	Fist fight
2D.	Forthright	2A.	Babe Ruth

3E.	Sea lion	3E.	Wrist watch
4B.	Living Room	4C.	Sunspot
5A.	Barn dance	5B.	Iced tea

No. 69		*No. 70*	
1D.	Teddy bear	1C.	Cheap skate
2B.	Pacemaker	2B.	Calm down
3E.	Cause trouble	3A.	Military aides
4C.	Stargazer	4E.	Nile Delta
5A.	Warehouse	5D.	Close shave

No. 71		*No. 72*	
1E.	Sweepstakes	1A.	Steer clear
2B.	Horselaugh	2E.	Forest fires
3A.	Watermelon	3B.	Stovepipe
4D.	Something	4C.	Form letter
5C.	South Pole	5D.	Kitchen sink

No. 73		*No. 74*	
1B.	Wasp nest	1C.	Human being
2C.	Toothbrush	2E.	Chicken coops
3E.	Gridiron	3B.	Skid Row
4A.	Raindrop	4D.	Shoe trees
5D.	Blank verse	5A.	Left turn

No. 75		*No. 76*	
1E.	Superman	1B.	Neon sign
2C.	Class ring	2D.	Sure-fire
3B.	Fireplug	3E.	Golf links
4A.	Still life	4C.	Tailspin
5D.	Sport coat	5A.	Tour bus

No. 77

1B. Spaceship
2C. Scalp lock
3A. Fiberglass
4E. Pest control
5D. Shoot out

No. 79

1E. Post office
2C. Standpoint
3A. Fort Worth
4B. Elbow grease
5D. Scarecrow

No. 78

1D. Race track
2B. Army camps
3C. Backbiter
4E. Serve time
5A. Horseshoe

No. 80

1B. Hurt pride
2D. Strip mining
3A. Staircase
4C. Three bears
5E. Trustworthy

Answers to Lost Letters Puzzles

5D   Dear—Beloved
6A   Alter—Change

No. 3

1A   Glad—Pleased
2F   Decay—Rot
3E   Girl—Maid
4C   Woo—Court
5B   Eat—Dine
6D   Dwell—Reside

No. 4

1D   Pace—Stride
2E   Close—Shut
3B   Wail—Howl
4A   Plump—Chubby
5C   Cut—Slash
6F   Old—Aged

No. 5

1F   Chum—Pal
2D   Give—Grant
3E   Boast—Brag
4B   Create—Build
5A   Hue—Tint
6C   Die—Decease

No. 6

1B   Tramp—Trudge
2E   Bold—Daring

3F   Trade—Swap
4D   Numerous—Many
5C   Past—Over
6A   Mix—Blend

No. 7

1D   Row—Brawl
2E   Burn—Char
3B   Dice—Cube
4F   Peel—Pare
5A   Earth—Planet
6C   Metal—Lead

No. 8

1A   Fine—Swell
2D   Swear—Curse
3E   Damp—Wet
4B   Anger—Wrath
5C   Wind—Twist
6F   Limb—Arm

No. 9

1C   Gather—Amass
2D   Yearn—Long
3F   Tear—Rip
4B   Ghost—Spirit
5A   Stop—Quit
6E   Tops—Best

No. 10

1E   Heat—Warm

2F   Alarm—Scare
3D   Act—Deed
4B   Ample—Sufficient
5C   Desire—Crave
6A   Frail—Weak

Answers to Regroup Puzzles

No. 1	No. 2
Latin American	Polecat
Foreign Legion	Bank vault
Jackknife	Patchwork
Pot shot	Bookworm
Pigpen	Nest egg
Pit stop	Headline
Sign language	Sidesaddle
Girl Scout	Boardwalk
Masterpiece	Vice president
Eyeball	Soapbox
Gamecock	Light switch
Gunboat	Green hornet

Yellowstone
Life jacket
Wallflower

Fish-hook
Cornbread
Squad car

No. 3

Fire alarm
Service station
Independent clause
Judgment Day
Grandfather clock
Back down
Stagecoach
Sunshine
Shut up
Football field
Handshake
Top secret
Light socket
Monkey wrench
Milk bottle

No. 4

Mailbag
Carrier pigeon
Little League
Rock Hudson
Rabbit punch
Sugar bowl
Major general
Electric train
Workman
Dishwasher
Peter Pan
Racetrack
Bay window
Footstool
Pine needle

No. 5

Red Sea
Skin cream
First aid
Handstand
Pocket money
Short order
Wildcat

No. 6

Safety razor
Tie pin
Toothbrush
Firecracker
Meeting place
Kickback
Soft touch

Shellfish

Treetop

Hatband

Postcard

Single file

West Point

Stop sign

Ice pick

Downtown

Household

Shoulder blade

Strapless

Ground hog

Jack Frost

Backbite

Play ball

No. 7

Right angle

Wormwood

Schoolteacher

Leap year

Bullfrog

Fight song

Oil drum

Beat eggs

Jet set

Plane geometry

Jump bail

Tightrope

Cutup

Bird bath

Outlay (Layout)

No. 8

Indian Ocean

Breezeway

Baby talk

Show business

Flatcar

Porthole

Trade wind

Icebreaker

Water moccasin

Manpower

Streamline

Spider monkey

Bookmark

Downright

Web-footed

No. 9

Buck private

House detective

Sawmill

No. 10

Price range

Freeze over

Red-hot

Gulf Stream

Coast Guard

Railroad

Jail cell

Bird dog

Software

Ball bearing

Trip hammer

Lockjaw

Bone-dry

Overdraw

Bloodhound

Cap pistol

Right Reverend

Graham cracker

Admiral Perry

Stonemason

Eyesight

Curb market

Rear guard

Hush money

Soda water

Puppy love

Letter opener

No. 11

No. 12

Landlady

Index finger

Top-heavy

Waistcoat

Pantyhose

Pipe dream

Haircut

Net weight

Newspaper

Cardboard

Footprint

Upside

Party line

Front yard

Home plate

Wellspring

Yellow fever

Shell game

In-laws

Galley slave

Proofread

Foreground

Stepfather

Tail wind

Millstone

Birthmark

Time bomb

Mastermind

Nevermore

Overwork

No. 13

Buck Rogers
Skin diver
Town house
Shipmate
Sweet potato
Bubble gum
Viceroy
President Cleveland
Roadrunner
Skyscraper
Creek Indians
Fishwife
Chip shot
Bathroom
Put up

No. 14

Purse strings
Body snatcher
Police dog
Pullman
Crab apple
Butterfly
Everything
Bellboy
Peppermint
Grasshopper
Carpet
Wood duck
Trademark
Cowcatcher
Fair play

No. 15

Silent night
Partnership
Yardstick
Rolling pin
Water main
Street dance
Colorblind
Alley cat

Bow out
Offside
Taillight
Popcorn
Square meal
Cross-eyed
Limestone

DATE DUE